This Is Not Normal

This Is Not Normal

The Politics of Everyday Expectations

Cass R. Sunstein

Yale UNIVERSITY PRESS

New Haven & London

Yale University Press books may be purchased in quantity for educational,
business, or promotional use. For information, please e-mail
sales.press@yale.edu (U.S. office) or sales@yaleup.co.uk (U.K. office).

Set in Janson type by Integrated Publishing Solutions.
Printed in the United States of America.

Library of Congress Control Number: 2020936929
ISBN 978-0-300-25350-4 (hardcover : alk. paper)

A catalogue record for this book is available from the British Library.

This paper meets the requirements of ANSI/NISO Z39.48-1992
(Permanence of Paper).

10 9 8 7 6 5 4 3 2 1

For Ellyn, Declan, and Rian, forever young

Contents

Contents

Preface

If your government jails people because of their political convictions, you might not think that it is so terrible if public officials read your email. If you live in a society in which officials routinely steal public money for their own use, you might not mind so much if an official asks for a little bribe in exchange for letting you open a small business. If sexual harassment is rampant in your society, you might not object much if male employers flirt with female employees. In a nation that suffers from pervasive poverty, the idea of a right to health care might not get much traction. What provokes our outrage depends on what surrounds us—on what we consider "normal."

Not so long ago, it was normal for public schools in the United States to require students to pray every morning. (As a young boy in public school in Massachusetts, I said the Lord's Prayer in school, Monday through Friday.) Not so long ago, it was normal for people to drive without seatbelts and to smoke in public buildings. Not so long ago, bans on same-sex marriage were part of life's furniture. Not so long ago, many people took democratic self-government so much for granted that it was not seen as needing justification. At the same time, they had a concrete understanding of what democratic self-government entailed, such that departures from that understanding were "not normal." They were essentially unthinkable.

In 2020, the coronavirus pandemic radically changed people's conception of what is normal. A ban on flying to Italy? At one point, that would have been unimaginable. Offices and shops closed, and schools and universities using online classes? At one point, people could not have tolerated those ideas. Staying at home, except for specified activities, such as getting food? That might have seemed the stuff of a nightmare, or perhaps authoritarianism. But in short order, all these became normal. Some people rebelled, but many people seemed to think: "Okay, I understand." As radical social changes were normalized, the number of people who were willing to agree to them, or even to embrace them, steadily grew.

What is normal might be either wonderful or horrible. The cry "This is not normal!" therefore needs to be supplemented by some argument if it is to be taken as synonymous with "This is terrible!" Some people try hard to expand the boundaries of the normal; others try to contract those boundaries. Without knowing what they are doing, we cannot know how to evaluate their actions. Freedom fighters try, simultaneously, to expand and contract the boundaries of what is normal. They seek to open some spaces and close others. Fascists and authoritarians of all stripes work to expand people's sense of what is normal—sometimes in stages, sometimes quite abruptly (consider the Holocaust). They also seek to contract that sense—suggesting, for example, that expressions of dissent and disagreement, once respected, are abhorrent, a kind of disloyalty, perhaps something to be forbidden. With the #MeToo movement and the attack on sexual violence and harassment, feminists have contracted the understanding of what is normal but also expanded it—for example, by suggesting that it is perfectly normal, or should be, to call harassers and rapists to account.

In this book, I shall explore the power of the normal from a variety of angles. Responses to a pandemic provide especially vivid examples, but I shall focus more generally on the relationship of the normal to the trials and tribulations of democracy—its creation, its improvement, its reformation, its deterioration, its collapse. As we will see, those who seek to promote democratic goals work hard to alter the sense of what is normal. They often suggest that if certain groups are denied a right to participate in politics or to say what they like, something has gone terribly wrong. We can see them as trying to enlarge people's understanding of the normal. They might alter the very meaning of the right to participate in politics—for example, by calling for automatic voter registration, for lowering the voting age, and for allowing convicted felons to vote. Movements for self-government, old and new, proceed in this way.

Those who seek to undermine democratic goals do something similar. They might suggest that certain restrictions on the right to vote, or on freedom of the press, are perfectly normal—the kind of thing that leaders simply do. Movements toward authoritarianism, old and new, proceed in this way. They might start slowly and move incrementally—an approach that, as we will see, can make good psychological sense. They might accelerate rapidly. As we will also see, that approach too can work if they have force on their side and can also move public opinion. Authoritarians might take advantage of any available opportunities, as happened in 2020, in both Hungary and Thailand, in connection with the coronavirus pandemic. When people are frightened, and need to take strong steps to protect public health, they might be diverted or open to any number of restrictions on their freedom.

These points cast a skeptical light on Winston Churchill's famous claim that "democracy is the worst form of government, except for all those other forms that have been tried from time to time." Churchill was clever, but his claim smacks of elitism. It seems to be a kind of sneer. Actually, it is a terrible thing to say. Democracy is not the least bad form of government; it is the best. This is so for two reasons. First, democracy is rooted in a commitment to the equal dignity of human beings. Because of that commitment, it is equally committed to people's right to govern themselves. Democrats insist that each of us is entitled to a voice in determining our nation's course. Democracy rests on a belief that sovereignty lies in the people, not a dictator, a monarch, a party, or a king. That belief depends in turn on a judgment that no person, and no group of people, should be subordinated to another.

Abraham Lincoln put it this way in 1854: "If the negro is a man, is it not to that extent, a total destruction of self-government, to say that he too shall not govern himself? When the white man governs himself that is self-government; but when he governs himself, and also governs *another* man, that is *more* than self-government—that is despotism.... No man is good enough to govern another man, without that other's consent. I say this is the leading principle—the sheet anchor of American republicanism."

The idea of a "sheet anchor" is a useful way of linking self-government, in people's individual capacities, with self-governance as a political ideal. A sheet anchor is no ordinary anchor. It is the most reliable one you have, the one least likely to fail under extreme stress. Lincoln was suggesting that if a culture embraces the idea of individual autonomy, its commitment to self-government will be secure.

Second, democracy is based on a recognition that self-governing institutions are likely to govern better and help people to enjoy better lives, simply because such institutions are highly responsive to the people. When public officials must stand for election, they have a strong incentive to focus on people's well-being. Whatever their status, they are made to be *servants*. Consider the remarkable finding by the economist Amartya Sen in his 1983 book titled *Poverty and Famines*, that in the history of the world, there has never been a famine in a system with a democratic press and free elections. Sen's starting point, which he demonstrates empirically, is that famines are a social product, not an inevitable result of food scarcity. Whether there will be a famine depends on people's "entitlements"—that is, what they are able to get. Even when food is limited, officials can allocate entitlements in such a way as to ensure that no one will starve.

But—and this is the crucial question—when will a government take the necessary steps to prevent starvation? The answer depends on that government's incentives. When there is a democratic system with free speech and a free press, the government is under intense pressure to ensure that people generally have access to food. And when officials are thus pressured, they respond. This is a point not merely about famines but about suffering of all kinds. It offers a significant lesson about the relationship between democracy and citizens' well-being. Popular control is no guarantee, of course, and no one should doubt that nondemocratic governments can perform very well. They have their own incentives, including retention of power, and to retain power, they need to respond to public distress. In 2020, the aggressive response of the Chinese government to the coronavirus epidemic, viewed by many as a success story, is a vivid illustration. But popular control increases the likelihood that government will actually serve people's interests and promote their well-being. If the people are sovereign, they are ultimately in charge.

Some people think there is a tension between democracy and human rights. After all, the latter operate as a check on the former. If people have rights, there are serious limits on what the democratic process can do to them. And indeed, there is such a thing as illiberal democracy—as, for example, when democracy leads to some kind of religious orthodoxy or widespread censorship. (Is that normal? History suggests that the answer isn't no.) The people might want to suppress freedom of speech, but if the nation respects the right to free speech, that right will stand in the people's way. It is tempting to think that full-blown democracy can compromise rights and that rights compromise democracy. But that is a terrible mistake, much worse than mere confusion.

As a matter of principle, democracy comes with its own internal morality, which includes a robust set of rights. Freedom of speech is certainly included: so are freedom of the press, the right to vote, religious liberty, and freedom of association. The principles that justify democracy—including the right to equal dignity and hence the right to help dictate the course of one's nation—call for rights of that kind. To be sure, we can debate the details. Some rights may not be included in democracy's internal morality; consider the right to sexual privacy. But there is no question that across a wide terrain, democracy and human rights march hand in hand. The justification for democracy is a justification of (some) human rights as well. In any democracy, a free press cannot be treated as an enemy of the people (and describing the press in that ugly and savage way expands, not for the better, the sense of what is normal).

Of course, the idea of democratic government can be understood in many ways, and many different systems can qualify as democratic. A parliamentary system is democracy; so is a presidential system. Different democracies have different understandings of rights, and that is fine. A democracy can insist on a large role for experts and expertise, or not; it can be highly technocratic, or not so much. (My own enthusiastic vote is in favor of experts and expertise, as we will see in chapter 7.) A democracy can be a *republic*, in the sense that it gives a great deal of authority to elected representatives rather than to the people themselves. We should be able to agree that many systems cannot be counted as democratic. But democracy is a pretty wide tent.

After World War II, the argument for democracy seemed secure, even overwhelming. A shining star, and an enduring example, was West Germany, with its iconic constitutional commitment in Article 1: "Human dignity shall be inviolable. To respect and protect it shall be the duty of all state authority." To be sure, billions of people lived under nondemocratic systems. During the Cold War, Soviet Communism posed a serious threat to democracies in Europe and North America. But in principle, democracy had the high moral ground. After the collapse of the Soviet Union, the issue seemed even more straightforward: democracy was best. It is a sign of its primacy that so many countries labeled themselves democracies and republics even when they were not: for example, the "German Democratic Republic" and the "People's Republic of Korea."

Admittedly, I am painting with a broad brush. No one should doubt that some societies can do well along important dimensions even if they are not democratic. Not long ago, I visited a nondemocratic nation, some of whose leaders asked me, in a private meeting and with genuine puzzlement, "How can democracies possibly plan? Don't things change too rapidly? Don't elections ruin the ability to govern well?" Those leaders struck me as both intelligent and decent, and they argued that their own system was intelligent and decent. I emphasized that democracies could do better because they are deeply informed by what citizens think. Their answer was immediate and unforgettable: "We agree! That's why we are constantly consulting the people, to see what they think!" Nondemocratic nations can be highly attentive to the views and concerns of citizens. We could also rank nations along a democratic continuum; some nations are only barely democratic. But I am making a simpler point. For the last decades of the twentieth century and a good chunk of the twenty-first, democracy was plainly ascendant.

To say the least, things are different now. Democracy is being tested in multiple ways. Its historical and social contingency is clear, as is its fragility. The idea of equal dignity is under siege from authoritarians of all kinds. In addition, and more fundamentally, many people do not believe that self-government can deliver the goods—that it can increase the likelihood that people's lives will go well.

I shall be exploring the power of the normal and democracy's trials from a variety of angles, all of which involve the creation and alteration of political norms, and changing conceptions of what counts as normal: the rise of authoritarianism in the 1930s; the dependence of our judgments—aesthetic, ethical, and political—on what else we see (and this may be the most fundamental point of all); the theory behind the American founding, which inspired Lincoln; constitutional amendments, which may mean or amount to a kind of refounding, and which are a way for democracy to revise itself; radicalism of multiple kinds; the "Who will stop me?" norm entrepreneurship of Ayn Rand; the nature and role of liberalism; and counterfactual history, which suggests the role of accident and serendipity in how things turn out.

If we examine the power of what is taken to be normal, we can better appreciate the contingency of democratic arrangements—and their fragility. Things can be very stable, or not. They can break down, at least to some extent, in a relative hurry. At the Virginia ratifying convention, James Madison, the most important figure behind the U.S. Constitution, put it this way: "I go on this great republican principle, that the people will have virtue and intelligence to select men of virtue and wisdom. Is there no virtue among us? If there be not, we are in a wretched situation. No theoretical checks—no form of government can render us secure. To suppose that any form of government will secure liberty or happiness without any virtue in the people, is a chimerical idea. If there be sufficient virtue and intelligence in the community, it will be exercised in the selection of these men. So that we do not depend on their virtue, or put confidence in our rulers, but in the people who are to choose them."

There is a lot to say, of course, about the word *virtue*. Whole books have been written on the topic. We should understand

Madison to be drawing on the tradition of civic republicanism, which emphasized not only citizens' rights but also their obligation to participate in public affairs, and to do so independently and with their critical faculties intact. The best defenses of democracy turn out to depend on that form of virtue. It is part and parcel of democracy's understanding of equal dignity. And it is a predicate for the idea that when democracy works well, it will increase the likelihood that people's lives will go well, too.

With its internal morality, democracy is the best form of government, including all those other forms that have been tried from time to time. It is a luxury, and a blessing, to be able to take it as normal.

This Is Not Normal

ONE

Howling with the Wolves

These are difficult days for liberal democracy. In terms of global influence, China may well have surpassed the United States. Russia is resurgent. Developments in Turkey, Poland, Hungary, and the Philippines have led to widespread talk of a "democratic recession." In many nations, freedom of speech is under assault. Journalists and others are being intimidated, jailed, hurt, and even killed because they are thought to threaten the regime. In important respects, the United States is in retreat, certainly in terms of its moral leadership and its willingness to promote democratic ideals.

In such a time, we might be tempted to try to learn something from earlier turns to authoritarianism, above all from the triumphant rise of the Nazis in Germany in the 1930s. The problem is that Adolf Hitler's regime was so horrifying, and so unthinkably barbaric, that to many people, it is not easily taken as analogous to contemporary threats and shifts, even in nations where authoritarianism is gaining a foothold. Many accounts of the period depict a barely imaginable series of events, a nation gone mad. That produces distance and even a kind of comfort. It is as if we are reading a dystopian science fiction novel in which Hitler is a character, not an actual figure from not-so-distant history.

But some depictions of Hitler's rise are intimate and personal. They focus less on historic figures, struggles for power, large events, state propaganda, murders, and war, and more on the details of individual lives. They help explain not only how people can participate in terrible things but also how they can stand by quietly, living fairly ordinary day-to-day lives, in the midst of them. For that reason, they offer lessons for people who now live in the midst of genuine horrors, but also and equally for those to whom horrors may never come but where democratic practices and norms are under severe pressure. They tell us something important about the fragility of democratic norms and the relationship between politics and ordinary life, even when the political order is losing its moorings.

Milton Mayer's 1955 classic, republished in 2017 with an afterword by Cambridge historian Richard Evans, was one of the first accounts of ordinary life under Nazism.[1] *They Thought They Were Free* is dotted with humor and written with an improbably light touch. It provides a jarring contrast to Sebastian Haffner's devastating, breathless, unfinished 1939 memoir, *Defying Hitler,* which gives a moment-by-moment, you-are-there feeling to Hitler's rise.[2] (The manuscript, discovered by Haffner's son after the author's death, was first published in Germany in 2000, where it caused an immediate sensation.) What distinguishes these two accounts is their sense of intimacy. They do not focus on historic figures making transformative decisions. They explore how people navigated their lives.

Haffner's real name was Raimund Pretzel. He used a pseudonym so as not to endanger his family while in exile in England. He was a journalist, not a historian or theorist, but he interrupts his riveting narrative to tackle a broad question: "What is history, and where does it take place?" Most works of history, he writes, give "the impression that no more than a few dozen people are involved, who happen to be 'at the helm of the ship of state' and whose deeds and decisions form what is called history." In Haffner's view, that is wrong. "We anonymous others" are not just "pawns in the chess game." On the contrary, the "most powerful dictators, ministers, and generals are powerless against the simultaneous mass decisions taken individually and almost unconsciously by the population at large." He insists on the importance of investigating "some very peculiar, very revealing, mental processes and experiences" involving "the private lives, emotions and thoughts of individual Germans."

A Whoop and a Holler

Mayer had the same aim. An American journalist of German descent, he tried to meet with Adolf Hitler in 1935. He failed, but he did travel widely in Nazi Germany. Stunned to discover a mass movement rather than the tyranny of a diabolical few, he concluded that his original plan was all wrong. His real interest was not in Hitler but in humanity—in people like himself, to whom "something had happened that had not (or at least not yet) happened to me and my fellow countrymen." In 1952 he returned to Germany to find out what made Nazism possible, and in the process to explore when and whether democracy could collapse into horror.

Mayer decided to focus on ten people, different in many respects but with one characteristic in common: they had all been members of the Nazi Party. Eventually they agreed to talk, accepting his explanation that as an American of German ancestry, he hoped to give the people of his nation a better understanding of Germany. Mayer was truthful about that and about nearly everything else. But he was not forthcoming about a central point: he did not tell them he was a Jew.

In the late 1930s—the period that most interested Mayer—his subjects were working as a janitor, a soldier, a cabinetmaker, an office manager, a baker, a bill collector, an inspector, a high school teacher, and a police officer. The tenth had been a high school student. All of them were male. None had occupied a position of leadership or influence. All of them referred to themselves as "wir kleine Leute" (we little people). They lived in Marburg, a university town situated on the river Lahn not far from Frankfurt.

Mayer talked with them over the course of a year under informal conditions—coffee, meals, and long, relaxed evenings. He became friends with each. As he put it, with evident surprise, "I *liked* them. I couldn't help it." They could be ironic, funny, and self-deprecating. Most of them enjoyed a joke that had originated in Nazi Germany: "What is an Aryan?" "An Aryan is a man who is tall like Hitler, blond like Goebbels, and lithe like Göring."

They also could be wise. Speaking of the views of ordinary people under Hitler, one of them asked, "Opposition? How would anybody know? How would anybody know what somebody else opposes or doesn't oppose? That a man *says* he opposes or doesn't oppose depends upon the circumstances, where, and when, and to whom, and just how he says it. And then you must still guess *why* he says what he says."

Mayer's friend was referring to the important idea of "preference falsification": People often fail to say what they like and think, at least in public, because of existing social norms (or official threats).[3] Preference falsification can be found everywhere, including in democracies. It is one reason that political orders, and any status quo, can be far more fragile than people think. When authoritarianism is gaining a foothold, preference falsification runs rampant. I will return to that problem in chapter 3.

When Mayer returned home, he was afraid for his own country. He felt "that it was not German Man that I had met, but Man," and that under the right conditions, he could easily have turned out as his German friends did. He learned that Nazism took over Germany not "by subversion from within, but with a whoop and holler." Many Germans "wanted it; they got it; and they liked it."

Mayer's most stunning conclusion is that with one partial exception (the teacher), none of his subjects "saw Nazism as we— you and I—saw it *in any respect.*" Whereas most of us understand Nazism as a form of tyranny, enslaving or murdering its citizens and violating human rights, Mayer's subjects "did not know before 1933 that Nazism was evil. They did not know between 1933 and 1945 that it was evil. And they do not know it now." Seven years after the war, they looked back on Hitler's prewar years as the best time of their lives.

Mayer offers an essential point: even when tyrannical governments do horrific things, outsiders tend to exaggerate their effects on the actual experiences of most people. Human beings focus on their own lives and "the sights that meet them in their daily rounds." Democratic norms can be undermined, or democracy can collapse, for just that reason. Nazism also made things better for the people Mayer interviewed—not (as many people think) because it restored some lost national pride but more concretely because it improved daily life. Germans who were not persecuted were able to vacation in Norway in the summer ("Strength through Joy"). They had jobs and better housing. Fewer people were hungry or cold, and the sick were more likely to receive treatment. The blessings of the New Order, as it was called, seemed to be enjoyed by "everybody."

Mayer's subjects liked and admired Hitler, even in retrospect. They saw him as someone with "a *feeling* for masses of people" who spoke directly in opposition to all aspects of the existing order: the government, the peace treaty, unemployment. They applauded Hitler for his rejection of "the whole pack"—"*all* the parliamentary politicians and *all* the parliamentary parties"— and for his "cleanup of moral degenerates." One of them described Hitler as "a spellbinder, a natural orator. I think he was carried away from truth, even from truth, by his passion. Even so, he always believed what he said."

Mayer did not bring up the topic of anti-Semitism with any of his subjects, but after a few meetings, each of them did so on his own, and they all returned to it constantly. When the local synagogue was burned in 1938, most of the community felt only one obligation: "*not to interfere.*" Eventually Mayer showed his friends an issue of the local newspaper from November 11, 1938, which contained the following report: "In the interest of their own security, a number of male Jews were taken into custody yesterday. This morning they were sent away from the city." None of them remembered seeing it, or indeed anything like it.

The killing of 6 million Jews? Fake news. Four of Mayer's friends insisted that the only Jews taken to concentration camps were traitors to Germany, and that the rest were permitted to leave with their property or its fair market value. The bill collector agreed that the killing of the Jews "was wrong, unless they committed treason in wartime. And of course they did." He added that "some say it happened and some say it didn't," and that you "can show me pictures of skulls . . . but that doesn't prove it." In any case, "Hitler had nothing to do with it." Another spoke similarly: "If it happened, it was wrong. But I don't believe it happened."

With evident fatigue, the baker reported, "One had no time to think. There was so much going on." His account tracked that of Mayer's colleague, a German philologist in the country at the time, who emphasized the devastatingly incremental nature of the descent into tyranny, explaining, "We had no time to think about these dreadful things that were growing, little by little, all around us." The philologist pointed to a regime bent on diverting its people through endless self-celebrations and dramas (often involving real or imagined enemies), and "the gradual habituation of the people, little by little, to being governed by surprise." In his account, "Each step was so small, so inconsequential, so well explained, or, on occasion, so 'regretted,'" that people could no more see the big picture "developing from day to day than a farmer in his field sees the corn growing. One day it is over his head."

How It Stank

Focusing largely on 1933, Haffner offers a radically different picture, in which the true nature of Nazism was evident and known to many Germans from the very start. Just twenty-five years old in that year, studying law with the goal of becoming a judge or administrator, Haffner catalogues the mounting effects of Nazism on the lives of his high-spirited friends and fellow students, preoccupied with fun, prospects, and love affairs. Haffner says that as soon as the Nazis took power, he was saved by his sense of smell: "As for the Nazis, my nose left me with no doubts. It was just tiresome to talk about which of their alleged goals and intentions were still acceptable or even 'historically justified' when all of it stank. How it stank! That the Nazis were enemies, my enemies and the enemies of all I held dear, was crystal clear to me from the outset."

A form of terror aimed at dissenters started early, as citizens were simultaneously distracted by an endless stream of festivities and celebrations. The combination produced a massive increase in fear, which led many skeptics to become Nazis. Nonetheless, people flirted, enjoyed romance, "went to the cinema, had a meal in a small wine bar, drank Chianti, and went dancing together." Sounding here like Mayer's subjects, Haffner writes that it was the "automatic continuation of ordinary life" that hindered "any lively, forceful reaction against the horror."

In Haffner's telling, the collapse of freedom and the rule of law occurred in increments, some of which seemed relatively insignificant. The point holds as well for the attacks on Jews. In 1933, when Nazi officers stood menacingly outside Jewish shops, Jews were merely "offended. Not worried or anxious. Just offended." But Haffner emphasizes that to him, Hitler's brutality and the coming politicization of everyday life were clear from the outset. In the early days of Hitler's regime, a self-styled republican advised Haffner to avoid skeptical comments because they were no use: "I think I know the fascists better than you. We republicans must howl with the wolves."

Haffner catalogues the howling. Books started to disappear from bookshops and libraries. Journals and newspapers disappeared as well, and those that remained kept to the party line.

As early as 1933, Germans who refused to become Nazis found themselves "in a fiendish situation: it was one of complete and unalleviated hopelessness; you were daily subjected to insults and humiliation."

Haffner sought refuge in the private domain, including a small group of young people studying law who had formed something like an intimate debating club. They were very good friends. One of the members, named Holz, held nationalistic views. Others disagreed, but it was all civil, the kind of energetic discussions young people have about politics. The group fell apart when Holz accused Haffner of "ignoring the monumental developments in the resurgence of the German people" and of being "a latent danger to the state"—and, ominously, threatened to denounce him to the Gestapo.

Haffner's narrative starts to break off toward the end of 1933, with a delicate and almost unbearably moving account of several idyllic weeks with the love of his life, who was engaged to an Englishman and who was about to leave Germany for good. Seeing his distress after informing him of her engagement, his lover responded with infinite gentleness: "But I'm here now." Summarizing those weeks and revealing something about human resilience, a passage close to the end of Haffner's unfinished manuscript comes from the poet Friedrich Hölderlin:

> Let us not look forward
> Nor back.
> Be cradled, as in
> A swaying boat on the sea.

Daily Life

Precisely because of the fine-grained, even intimate nature of their accounts, Mayer and Haffner speak directly to those concerned about what makes democracies vulnerable. To be sure, readers can't know whether to believe Mayer's subjects when they claim ignorance of what Hitler actually did. (Mayer isn't sure either.) But they are convincing when they say that they were mostly focused on their families, their friends, and their daily lives. Haffner's depiction of the "automatic continuation of daily life," possible for so many amid their government's step-by-step assault on freedom and dignity, is in the same vein.

These narratives offer large and enduring lessons. Turkey, for example, has been sliding toward authoritarianism through the standard tactics—jailing political dissidents, limiting freedom of speech, treating critics as enemies of the state, and obliterating checks and balances. It's important to emphasize that under President Donald Trump, the United States remains a democracy; it has not slid into authoritarianism. Trump has been more bark than bite. But he has not been *only* bark, and barks matter, if only because they make a mockery of essential political norms and prepare the way for worse.

If the president of the United States is constantly lying, refusing to respond to subpoenas in connection with an impeachment inquiry, asking foreign officials to investigate political opponents, complaining that the independent press is responsible for "fake news," threatening to withdraw licenses from television networks, publicly demanding jail sentences for political opponents, undermining the authority of the Department of Justice and the Federal Bureau of Investigation, magnifying social divisions, sowing hatred and fear along racial and religious lines, delegitimating critics as "crooked" or "failing," and refusing, in violation of the law, to protect young children against the risks associated with lead paint—well, it's hardly Adolf Hitler, but it's nothing the United States has seen before.[4] Things are still worse if opposition to violation of long-standing norms is limited to the Democratic Party, and if Republicans applaud, agree, laugh, make excuses—or howl with the wolf.

Many Americans who lack enthusiasm for Trump nonetheless see him as having "a *feeling* for masses of people" and as "carried away from truth, even from truth, by his passion." Like many Germans in the 1930s, they think that the enemy of my enemy is my friend—which means that they are happy to focus only or mostly on what they see as deplorable among Trump's critics. They may not be pro-Trump, but they are anti-anti-Trump. That's cowardly. It's also dangerous.

Habituation, confusion, distraction, self-interest, fear, rationalization, and a sense of personal powerlessness make terrible things possible. They call attention to the importance of individual actions, both small and large, by people who never get into the history books.

But Haffner offered something like a corollary, which is that the ultimate safeguard against aspiring authoritarians, and wolves of all kinds, lies in individual conscience—in "decisions taken individually and almost unconsciously by the population at large."

TWO

The New Normal

George Orwell's *1984* is unquestionably the greatest fictional account of authoritarianism—the most astute, the most precise, the most attuned to human psychology.[1] One of its defining chapters explores the Two Minutes Hate, which helps establish and maintain Big Brother's regime. As Orwell describes it, the Hate begins with a flash of a face on a large screen. It is Emmanuel Goldstein, the Enemy of the People. Goldstein produces fear and disgust. He was once a leader in the Party, but he abandoned it and became a counterrevolutionary. Condemned to death, he managed to escape and to disappear. "He was the primal traitor, the earliest defiler of the Party's purity," ultimately responsible for heresies and treacheries of all kinds. In the first thirty seconds of the Hate, Goldstein's voice is heard denouncing the Party and calling for freedom.

The result is immediate rage and fear in the audience. Somehow Goldstein has managed to remain a serious threat. Wherever he is, he commands a shadow army, a network of conspirators. He is the author of a terrible book, endorsing all of the heresies.

In the second minute of the Hate, people become frenzied. They leap and shout, trying to drown out Goldstein's maddening voice. Children join in the shouting. Orwell's hero, Winston, finds himself unable to resist. He too begins to shout, and also to kick violently. This is no mere show on his part. "The horrible thing about the Two Minutes Hate was not that one was obliged to act a part, but that it was impossible to avoid joining in." No pretense is necessary: "A hideous ecstasy of fear and vindictiveness, a desire to kill, to torture, to smash faces with a sledgehammer, seemed to flow through the whole group of people like an electric current, turning one even against one's will into a grimacing, screaming lunatic."

Despite loathing Big Brother, Winston notices his feelings changing "into adoration, and Big Brother seemed to tower up, an invincible, fearless protector, standing like a rock" against the threat posed by Goldstein. And as his hatred mounts, it turns sexual. Winston fantasizes about raping and murdering the girl behind him.

At that point, the Hate rises to its climax. Goldstein's voice becomes that of an actual bleating sheep, and for a moment, his face on the screen is transformed into that of a sheep. Big Brother's face then fills the screen, powerful, comforting, and mysteriously calm. Big Brother's actual words are not heard but they are felt, a kind of reassurance. Then the Party's three slogans appear on the screen:

WAR IS PEACE
FREEDOM IS SLAVERY
IGNORANCE IS STRENGTH

A member of the audience seems to pray to Big Brother. For thirty seconds the audience chants in his honor, in "an act of self-hypnosis, a deliberate drowning of consciousness by means of rhythmic noise." Winston chants with the rest, for "it was impossible to do otherwise."

The Two Minutes Hate is a distillation of a common tactic of authoritarian leaders. They focus attention on enemies and heretics—those who seek to destroy society's fabric. For Hitler, of course, it was the Jews. What makes the Two Minutes Hate so insidious is that even those who oppose it and see it for what it is cannot easily resist it. The sheer repetition of an accusation—against Emmanuel Goldstein, Jews, Muslims, immigrants, Hillary Clinton, or the press—makes it difficult not to feel, in some part of one's soul, that the accusation is correct. Even if one believes that Goldstein is innocent, ineffective, benign, or dead, the Hate gets under one's skin.

It is hard not to hate Goldstein.

The Power of the Normal

In politics, what counts as morally unacceptable behavior? Is the Two Minutes Hate abhorrent? How did people come to accept and even embrace it? How do people decide whether political behavior is morally fine, morally troublesome, or morally intolerable? What is beyond the pale?

A large part of the answer lies in what is taken to be normal. That answer tells us, in turn, about when democratic governments, or the norms that support them, can become fragile in short periods. Drawing on psychological research, I will suggest, first, that as mandates and behavior in general get worse, things that were once seen as bad or even as terrible may come to be seen as mildly distasteful or even fine. Call this *opprobrium contraction*. That certainly happened in Germany under Hitler, and to a significant extent it is happening in the United States under Donald Trump. It is also what happened all over the world in connection with the coronavirus epidemic of 2020. I will suggest, second, that as behavior in general improves, actions that were previously seen as fine or as mildly distasteful may come to seem bad or terrible. Call this *opprobrium expansion*. In many democracies, that happens as well. Consider the expanding concern with civil rights violations, including sexual harassment.

My central concern is opprobrium contraction. As burdensome mandates or constraints, and norm-violating or horrific conduct, increase and come to be seen as pervasive, cases of objectionable behavior might not encounter much public opprobrium. The rise of authoritarianism contains many examples. Or suppose, more generally, that norm violations by a nation's leader become widespread, and that some of those violations are egregious, even violations of human rights. Suppose people experience the Two Minutes Hate or something close to it. A "new normal" has been established that might cause opprobrium to contract. At many points in recent history, opprobrium expansion and opprobrium contraction have been observed in practice. With these claims, I hope to say something about extremism, responses to pandemics, the fragility of democratic norms, conformity, the rule of law, authoritarianism, and what is not quite visible.

Let us begin with a research paper by a team of psychologists led by David Levari, who focused on what they call "prevalence-induced concept change."[2] As they note, many of our judgments are quite stable and should not be expected to shift in response to what else we see. This is meant as an empirical claim. For example, a doctor's judgment about whether someone has a brain tumor, diabetes, or heart disease ought not to depend on other people's medical conditions. A brain tumor is a brain tumor, regardless of how prevalent brain tumors are in the population. A field goal is a field goal and a double fault is a double fault, even if many kickers are making field goals and even if many players are double faulting. In that respect, human judgments are often independent of the social context.

But some of our most important judgments turn out to depend on what is prevalent. *What we see, with respect to some object X, depends on what else we see.* Let us bracket the question of whether and when that is a problem, whether and when it leads to mistakes, and how it connects to democracy and politics. For the moment, it should be seen as a simple claim of fact.

To investigate that claim, Levari et al. engaged in some simple experiments, mostly involving the perception of color. In their principal test, they showed participants a thousand dots on a continuum from very purple to very blue, asking them to decide whether each dot was blue or purple. After two hundred trials, they decreased the number of clearly blue dots for about half of the participants. As the number of clearly blue dots was reduced, those participants became significantly more likely to categorize dots as blue! They started to "see" dots as blue that had previously looked purple. By contrast, those participants who saw a constant number of blue dots did not shift in their judgments.

Why did people who saw fewer clearly blue dots start to categorize more dots as blue? Why did they start to see dots that they had previously seen as purple as blue? The reason should not be obscure. Suppose a dot is on the border between blue and purple. If people are seeing a lot of very or clearly blue dots, that borderline dot will look purple. It is certainly less blue than what they are seeing. It might not look blue at all. Once the number of clearly blue dots is reduced, borderline blue dots begin to look bluer by comparison. People will start to see them as blue.

Levari et al. found the same effect even when people were explicitly informed that the number of clearly blue dots would "definitely decrease" over trials. Importantly, they replicated their findings even when people were explicitly instructed to "be consistent" and not to allow their concept of blue to change over the trials—and even when the people given these instructions were offered a monetary incentive to follow them. That is powerful evidence that people's perceptions changed with changes in the context, or more particularly, with changes in what was prevalent or normal.

In another experiment, Levari et al. *increased* the number of clearly blue dots over the trials. As that happened, participants became more likely to see dots as purple—including dots of the same color that they had earlier categorized as blue. It is worth underlining this finding. It suggests that an *increase* in the prevalence of some object can *decrease* the likelihood that people will see a somewhat contrasting object as belonging in the same general category.

Are these findings generalizable? Do they have implications for moral, political, and legal judgments? What does it mean, broadly, to say that concepts change as prevalence changes? Levari et al. tested these questions by showing people a series of eight hundred computer-generated human faces and asking them to say whether the faces looked threatening or not. Their central finding is that *whether people see human faces as threatening depends on what other faces they are seeing.* When the number of very threatening faces was reduced, people started to see faces as threatening that they did not previously see that way at all. A formerly benign face—or a face that was benign enough—starts to look scarier when we do not see a lot of clearly threatening faces.

Whether a color counts as blue is not a moral question, and it does not have a clear implication for policy or law. Whether a face counts as threatening is perhaps more relevant to citizens, police officers, politicians, lawyers, and judges. And Levari et al. offered a final experiment addressing a more directly relevant question: what counts as ethical? More particularly, they asked people to act as reviewers for an institutional review board (IRB). The purpose of an IRB is to decide whether a proposed research proposal violates ethical standards. For example, an experiment that subjects people to torture could not possibly receive IRB approval. By contrast, a survey of people's views about fuel economy labels would probably be approved, so long as anonymity was assured. Most proposals fall between these extremes.

Levari et al. showed people 240 proposals and asked them to decide whether the studies should be allowed to go forward as ethical. Independent raters—not participants in the experiments—had previously placed the proposals on a continuum from very ethical to very unethical. The design was exactly the same as for dots and faces, and so was the result. After ninety-six trials, the number of clearly unethical proposals was decreased for half of the participants. As that number decreased, people became significantly more likely to reject proposals that were ethically ambiguous. In other words: when clearly unethical proposals are pervasive, proposals that are questionable but not clearly unethical are more likely to be approved than when clearly unethical proposals are less common. A reduction in the number of clearly unethical proposals makes people more likely to disapprove of proposals that had formerly looked acceptable.

It is eminently reasonable to suppose that if the number of clearly unethical proposals were increased, people would begin to approve of proposals that had formerly looked unacceptable. There is a large lesson here. If people are surrounded by conduct that is morally abominable, or seeing a lot of it, they will not disapprove of, and may even be fine with, conduct that is morally bad (but not abominable). That is the power of the normal: our moral judgments are often a product of what else we see, and when what we see is very, very bad, we might not disapprove of the bad, or even the very bad. We might see it as fine, or even as good.

When Prevalence Matters

The mechanism behind these findings and their boundary conditions need to be clarified. Suppose people are asked to say whether numbers are higher or lower than five, whether lines are longer or shorter than one inch, whether a picture has more or fewer than two people in it, or whether an animal is a horse or a wolf. We would not expect prevalence to matter. Even if you see a lot of horses, a wolf is a wolf. There are well-defined absolute criteria governing numbers, lengths, and the difference between horses and wolves; the criteria answer all questions and are easy to apply. For that reason, judgments ought not to be affected by what is prevalent.

Other judgments are made without well-defined absolute criteria; some of these judgments are inevitably comparative and thus relative to what else we see. Suppose people are asked to say whether faces are attractive, whether colors are dark, whether people are tall, whether buildings are high, whether behavior is hateful or racist, or whether judicial opinions, legal briefs, examinations, or essays are well written. They will likely have some sense of what falls inside and outside of these categories, such that many judgments are obvious and will be unaffected by what is prevalent. Some faces are just threatening; some colors are clearly blue. But other judgments are not at all obvious, which means that they would almost certainly be affected by the other faces, colors, heights, behavior, and writing people are seeing. That is certainly true of judgments about the behavior of public officials, including prime ministers and presidents, and it may be true about mandates (such as those associated with a pandemic or with an authoritarian government).

Of course, we could imagine establishing, even for such questions, sufficiently well-defined criteria whose meaning is clear independent of context. Such criteria would make prevalence irrelevant or far less relevant. They might operate as rules. But for attractiveness, darkness, and height, whether behavior is hateful or racist, or whether essays are well written, such criteria generally do not exist in the human mind (even though some cases are easily included or excluded).

Similar conclusions hold for whether a color is blue, whether a face is threatening, and whether a proposal is ethical. People lack sufficiently well-defined, absolute criteria that would make context and prevalence irrelevant. Here too, many cases are easy and thus unaffected by what else people see. But when the criteria people use are not well defined, judgments will often be an artifact of what other cases they see or have in mind. Those cases will form the reference point against which hard cases are resolved. They might also make some cases hard and other cases easy.

What's Better?

We should stipulate that certain colors are unambiguously blue and others are unambiguously purple. We might even identify clear criteria to distinguish blue from purple. In principle, scientists might be able to specify something about vision, such that a clear line separates the two. Armed with these criteria, we should be able to say under what circumstances people start to err— perhaps with many very blue dots, perhaps with some, perhaps with none.

The same might be said about threatening faces. If we had objective criteria by which to measure threateningness, we could specify the circumstances in which people's judgments go right or wrong. Something similar (and essential) might be said about ethical research proposals. Ideally, there would be clear criteria to allow authorities to distinguish the ethical from the unethical. In principle, institutional review boards should be armed with such criteria, so that they would not make different judgments depending on what kinds of proposals they happen to have seen recently. Indeed, something like that may be so in practice, at least in some institutions. Clear rules reduce the risk of prevalence-induced change in judgments, simply because rules leave people with less discretion when they are making those judgments. By contrast, vague standards invite shifts in judgments in accordance with shifts in prevalence.

We could go further. Some people might be experts on what really is blue. Because they have criteria, or something like a formula, they can distinguish blue from purple in a fairly consistent way. They operate with the help of something like a rule. Some people might similarly be experts on what kinds of faces are threatening. Blueness experts and threatening-face experts might be matched by ethical experts, and none of them should be influenced, or susceptible to influence, by what is pervasive. We might go further still. In principle, any kind of judgment could be disciplined by criteria or by a formula—effectively a rule—and if so, what else is in the foreground or background ought not to matter.

But suppose that people lack well-defined criteria or any kind of formula. Suppose that they use an open-ended standard. In the abstract, there is no reason to think judgments will be either better or worse in circumstances in which something is prevalent— very blue dots, very threatening faces, highly unethical proposals. Normative criteria are needed to answer that question. To know whether people are making mistakes, such criteria are indispensable. But my main point is empirical rather than normative: judgments may shift unless such criteria are in place. For current purposes, two phenomena should be kept in mind. As prevalence *decreases*, more cases will seem to fit within the category. As prevalence *increases*, fewer cases will seem to fit within the category. Both phenomena carry promise as well as risk. Among other things, they help explain the growth and collapse of social norms.

More and Less

For many questions in morality, law, and politics, people are equipped with concepts like democracy, freedom, fairness, and equality. They know that cases can be aligned on a continuum, and that concepts are different from one another. But they lack anything like absolute, well-defined criteria for making relevant distinctions. To that extent, their judgments can be akin to judgments about what is blue, what is threatening, and what is ethical. People's judgments may be labile and endogenous to context. In the most extreme cases, the criteria themselves shift, even if the concept does not. What was once unacceptable is now normal, and vice versa. (Consider the coronavirus of 2020.) What is understood to be an intolerable restriction on freedom, or horrible conduct in one or another domain, becomes less or more prevalent over time; public judgments about other cases change accordingly.

The rise and fall of democratic norms can easily be understood in this light. In fact the accounts of ordinary life in Nazi Germany that we discussed in chapter 1 can readily be seen as case studies: as democratic norms started to weaken, eventually the horrific became the new normal. The rising attacks on Jews— beginning with relatively small and symbolic steps, culminating in the Holocaust—are a searing illustration. But we can see the same thing in much more modest form. In the second decade of the twenty-first century, pressure on democratic norms in Europe and the United States has led people to accept, and essentially to yawn at, actions and statements that would have been unacceptable a decade earlier.

That is a tale of opprobrium contraction, to which I will return shortly. With respect to opprobrium expansion, one lesson is simple: *Society can be an epistemic victim of its own successes.* We might fail to see the progress we have made. If a nation is more democratic than it once was, or if it has made serious dents in major social problems, its citizens might not recognize what has happened because they view existing problems in the new and improved context that they themselves have helped bring about. In the context of poverty, crime, and racial equality, for example, people might end up thinking that things have gotten worse— even if they are much better.

In a sense, it is *because* things have gotten so much better that people see them as worse. Changing norms and values focus public attention on issues that had once been neglected. In some nations, a crucial dimension along which things have gotten better is (say) that fewer people are poor, partly because the problem of poverty has received widespread attention. When this is so, the highly visible fact that some or many people are (still) poor—highly visible because of the attention given to the problem of poverty—might seem entirely unacceptable. Changing norms and values are responsible both for the reduction in prevalence and for the attention paid to the problems that remain.

We can stipulate that an error of fact is being made, but the overall evaluation is not simple. By hypothesis, things have become much better, but people do not see that, which is not ideal. Even so, there might be an important benefit: the remaining misconduct or hardship might be genuinely terrible, even if it is much less bad than what preceded it. If so, it might not be so bad if people think, "This is a problem and an injustice, and we need to do something about it," rather than, "Well, it's a lot better compared to before." There might be a kind of moral learning, in accordance with which conduct that was once forgiven or outcomes that did not trigger outrage are no longer tolerated (in part because the more egregious comparison cases are gone or rare). When opprobrium expands, we might want to applaud because opprobrium is justified.

With respect to opprobrium contraction, there is a corollary: *Society can be an epistemic victim of its own failures.* As norms fail or disintegrate, people may not understand the extent to which their moral and political commitments have collapsed. If things are actually getting worse, people might not appreciate that, or they might not see it clearly. That point helps to explain how norms break down. It also helps to explain public acquiescence in the face of cruel and vicious political acts, even horrors. We can easily see the phenomenon of opprobrium contraction in light of the research I have outlined. As the number of very blue dots increases, people start to see dots as purple that they had formerly seen as blue.

In such cases, the moral evaluation is not difficult. By stipulation, the underlying acts are cruel and vicious, even horrors. If people do not see them as such, something has gone terribly wrong. We can therefore offer a prediction: in periods in which unquestionably terrible acts are becoming more common, less terrible (but still terrible) acts will not be seen as terrible at all. They will look purple when in fact they are blue. In some cases, it is good if opprobrium contracts, but not if the dots really are blue.

THREE

Revolution Is in the Air

Why does large-scale political change happen? Why is it so hard to anticipate? Why does it seem to come out of nowhere? Why do shifts occur, both toward and away from democracy? Why and when do people change their behavior so quickly?

To vindicate the premise of these questions: in the 1930s, almost no one expected the rise of Nazism. Lenin was stunned by the success and speed of the Russian Revolution.[1] Tocqueville reported that no one foresaw the French Revolution. The Iranian Revolution of 1979 was largely unforeseen. More recently, the Arab Spring was unanticipated by many of the best analysts in the United States, the United Kingdom, and elsewhere.[2] Puzzlingly, large-scale political shifts, no matter their direction, seem to come in waves; they spread rapidly within and across countries, for reasons that remain unclear. It is tempting, and not unhelpful, to speak of demonstration and contagion effects.

But what exactly do those terms mean? In what sense is revolution, or some kind of revolt, "contagious"?

Much of the answer, I suggest, lies in three factors: preference falsification, diverse thresholds, and interdependencies.[3] Often all three go together; sometimes the latter two are sufficient. I will introduce complications in due course, but these three factors tell us much of what we need to know.

Preference Falsification

Preference falsification exists when people conceal, or do not reveal, what they actually prefer. They might hate immigrants and immigration, for example, but only in secret. They might say they believe in democracy even though they do not. They might have suffered from what they consider terrible wrongdoing, but they might not tell anyone. They might say they like the existing regime when they despise it. They might silence themselves. Their friends and neighbors might have no idea what they actually think.

To that extent, people live in a world of *pluralistic ignorance*, in which they do not know about the preferences of other people.[4] Under regimes that are oppressive (in one or another respect), preference falsification is common, making it difficult to learn what people actually think. But even in democracies, preference falsification is pervasive. Social norms prevent people from saying what they believe. People have a voice inside their head, and it might even be loud, but they do not let others know what it is saying.

The problem is that social norms, or perhaps the law, can drive a wedge between private and public preferences. The law matters if citizens lack freedom of speech and if dissent is punished. Social norms matter if people will be ostracized or punished, in some sense, if they reveal their likes, dislikes, hidden prejudices, anger, indignation, or dissatisfaction. Perhaps they will be shunned; perhaps powerful people will hurt them in some way; perhaps their employment prospects will be compromised. In any of these cases, people might not merely silence themselves, they might claim to be happy with the status quo when they are not. Consider some chilling words from a computer programmer from Syria: "When you meet somebody coming out of Syria for the first time, you start to hear the same sentences. That everything is okay inside Syria, Syria is a great country, the economy is doing great. . . . It'll take him like six months, up to one year, to become a normal human being, to say what he thinks, what he feels. Then they might start . . . whispering. They won't speak loudly. That is too scary. After all that time, even outside Syria you feel that someone is listening, someone is recording."[5]

The situation in Syria was of course distinctive, but something similar can happen in all nations, at least in some form. Leonardo Bursztyn of the University of Chicago, Georgy Egorov of Northwestern University, and Stefano Fiorin of UCLA tried to test whether President Donald Trump's political success affected Americans' willingness to support, in public, a xenophobic organization.[6] Two weeks before the election, Bursztyn and his col-

leagues recruited 458 people from eight states that the website
Predictwise said Trump was certain to win: Alabama, Arkansas,
Idaho, Nebraska, Oklahoma, Mississippi, West Virginia, and
Wyoming. Half the participants were told that Trump would
win their state. The other half received no information about
the likely election results.

All participants were then asked an assortment of questions,
including whether they would authorize the researchers to do-
nate $1 to the Federation for American Immigration Reform,
accurately described as an anti-immigrant organization whose
founder has written, "I've come to the point of view that for
European-American society and culture to persist requires a
European-American majority, and a clear one at that." Half the
participants were assured that their decision to authorize a donation would be anonymous. The other half were given no such
assurance. On the contrary, they were told that members of the
research team might contact them, suggesting that their willingness to authorize the donation could become public.

For those who were not informed about Trump's expected victory in their state, giving to the anti-immigration group was far
more attractive when anonymity was assured: 54 percent authorized the donation under cover of secrecy, as opposed to 34 percent when the donation might become public. But for those who
were told that Trump would likely win, anonymity did not matter at all. About half were willing to authorize the donation regardless of whether they were promised anonymity. Information
about Trump's expected victory altered the perception of social

norms, making many people more willing to allow their support for an anti-immigrant organization to become public knowledge.

Bursztyn and his colleagues repeated their experiment in the same states during the first week after Trump's election. They found that Trump's victory also eliminated the preference for anonymity—again, about half the participants authorized the donation regardless of whether it would be public. The general conclusion is that if Trump had not come on the scene, many Americans would refuse to authorize what might become a publicly known donation to an anti-immigrant organization, even if they were willing to give anonymously. But with Trump as president, people felt liberated. Trump's election apparently weakened the social norm against supporting anti-immigrant groups. It became more acceptable to be known to agree "that for European-American society and culture to persist requires a European-American majority, and a clear one at that."

This experiment has significant implications. When norms begin to loosen, people start to say what they actually think. They may conceal their xenophobia when they believe norms require them to do so. But when they receive a signal that norms are shifting, they are free to act and speak as they wish. Racism, sexism, and antidemocratic sentiments can be unleashed. It is also true, of course, that views about racial and sexual equality, and enthusiasm for democracy, can be unleashed in exactly the same way. Here, then, is another sense in which people's judgments about what is normal can affect what happens. The perceived normal can silence people, or it can give them a green light.

Diverse Thresholds

Whatever they think, different people require different levels of social support before they will reject the status quo or disclose what they actually believe.[7] Some might require no support at all; they are actors or rebels by nature. They might be courageous, committed, or foolhardy. Call them the zeroes (because they need zero support in order to act or speak out). They might turn out to be isolated; no one may join them, in which case they might look radical, foolish, even crazy. Other people might require a little support. They will not move unless someone else does, but if someone does, they are prepared to rebel as well. Call them the ones.

Others might require more than a little; they are the twos. The twos will do nothing unless they see the zeroes and the ones act first, but if the zeroes and ones rebel, they will too. The twos are followed by the threes, and the fours, and the tens, and the hundreds, thousands, all the way up to the infinites (those who will not oppose the regime no matter what). We can see these stylized numbers as applying to social movements involving Nazism, Brexit, Black Lives Matter, and climate change. We can also see them as applying to people who decided to wear masks in public in response to the coronavirus pandemic of 2020.

Outside of science fiction, it is not possible to see people's thresholds. People may not quite know whether they themselves are twos, threes, fours, or tens. They might be surprised. Consider the words of John Adams, writing with evident amazement about the American Revolution: "Idolatry to Monarchs, and servility to Aristocratical Pride, was never so totally eradicated from so many Minds in so short a Time."[8] Thomas Paine put it this way: "Our style and manner of thinking have undergone a revolution more extraordinary than the political revolution of a country. We see with other eyes; we hear with other ears; and think with other thoughts, than those we formerly used."[9]

Adams and Paine were right to be amazed, but I am offering a friendly amendment to their account. Many people did not really idolize monarchs, and their eyes and ears were not "other." As social norms shifted, they felt free to declare what they actually thought. That helped make the American Revolution possible.

Interdependencies

Interdependencies point to the fact that the behavior of the ones, the twos, the threes, and so forth will depend crucially on *who is seen to have done what.* Imagine the various citizens in a kind of temporal queue. The zeroes go first, then the ones, the twos, the threes, and so forth; or perhaps vice versa; or perhaps it is all random. Under imaginable assumptions, a rebellion will occur, but *only given the right distribution of thresholds and the right kind of visibility.*[10] If the ones see the zeroes, they will rebel, and if the twos see the ones, they too will rebel, and if the threes see the twos, they will join them. If the conditions are just right, almost everyone will rebel.

But the conditions have to be just right. Suppose there are no zeroes, or that no one sees them. If so, no rebellion will occur. And if there are few ones, the regime is likely to be safe. If most people are tens or hundreds or thousands, the same is true, even if there are some ones, twos, threes, and fours.

We should now be able to identify three reasons why political systems may be more fragile than they appear, and also why large-scale political change is impossible to predict. First, we do not know what people's preferences are. By hypothesis, they cannot be observed. Second, we do not know what people's thresholds are. Those too are unobservable. Third, we cannot anticipate social interactions—who will say or do what, and when, and who will see them. It is important to emphasize the third point. Even if we could identify people's preferences and specify their thresholds, we would not be able to predict their social interactions. The point bears on social movements of all kinds. In the case of oppressive societies, it may be possible to know that people are widely miserable or dissatisfied; in the context of sexual assault and sexual harassment, it is reasonable to assume that dissatisfaction is widespread. But that is not enough.

These points suggest that even if new technologies make it increasingly possible to identify private preferences—for example, by exploring people's online behavior—we could not predict revolutions.[11] To be sure, we would know something important: a revolution is more likely if people secretly hate the regime. But while secret opposition may be necessary for revolution, it is not sufficient. To know what will happen, we would need to know people's thresholds as well, and obtaining that knowledge is difficult or impossible. And even if we overcame that challenge, we would need to know who interacts with whom, who sees whom, and when. No one has that kind of prescience. But the answers to those questions may well determine outcomes.

These points help explain not only why large-scale social movements are unpredictable but also why they are often sparked by seemingly small, random events—who did what when, or who heard what when, or whether a butterfly flapped its wings at the right moment. We might think that a practice or a regime was bound to fall, but it really was not. It *happened* to fall. The same is true if it does not fall. It *happened* not to fall.

Complications

This very simple account needs to be complicated in several ways. First, *revisions of norms can construct new preferences and values rather than unleash suppressed ones.* New norms, and laws that entrench or fortify them, can give rise to beliefs, preferences, and values that did not exist before. Authoritarians may benefit from new norms; often they are *norm entrepreneurs.* The same is true of those who are committed to democratic self-government. They might not be trying to overcome preference falsification at all. Efforts to respond to pandemics by directing people to wash their hands and to stay home are efforts to construct new values, not to unleash existing ones.

Second, people's preferences may adapt to the status quo.[12] They might not have to work hard to shut themselves up. They might not even think that the status quo is bad, because they are used to it. Consider these words from a woman in North Korea: "It never occurred to me that I could or would want to do any-

37

thing about it. It was just how things are."[13] The most important word here is *want*. To be sure, fully adaptive preferences are an extreme case, even under conditions of real fear. It might be better to speak of *partially adaptive preferences*, in which people are aware that something is wrong or bad or horrific, but their awareness takes the form of a small voice in the head, to which they do not pay a great deal of attention. But the idea of preference *falsification* is too simple when people's preferences are an artifact of the status quo. Whether we are dealing with preference falsification, adaptive preferences, or partially adaptive preferences cannot be answered in the abstract.

Third, the very word *preferences* is under-descriptive or perhaps misleading. It might be better to speak of people's beliefs, experiences, or values. Under an oppressive regime, people might believe that terrible injustices are committed or that their values are being violated. They might have seen those injustices firsthand. They might have been the object of them—arrest, detention, imprisonment, rape, torture. To be sure, they are also concealing or falsifying what they prefer, but that is hardly an adequate account of what is happening. They are not merely concealing or falsifying their deepest convictions. If they are themselves victims, they are concealing or even falsifying *what actually happened to them*. (Talk about fake news.)

Fourth, and crucially, rebels do not undertake a full analysis of the costs and benefits of rebellion. They rely on mental shortcuts, or heuristics, in deciding what to do when. For that reason, available incidents or outcomes might affect probability judgments.[14] If a town suddenly falls to rebels, or if a government collapses, other rebels might believe that the probability of success is high. The availability heuristic, as it is called, works with emphatically social forces, producing *availability cascades*, as specific incidents or results move rapidly from one person to another, altering judgments about what is likely to happen.[15] A revolutionary movement might be fueled or halted by an availability cascade.

Fifth, fate is not only in the hands of revolutionaries. There is also the regime, there are counterrevolutionaries, and there may well be counterrevolution. As a revolutionary cascade starts to develop, the regime is likely to react. It might, for example, try to entrench pluralistic ignorance by hiding or preventing visible rebellion or mass demonstrations. It might allow dissent and disagreement—until they become too visible. It might make concessions, hoping to retain power. It might try to dissuade the hundreds and the thousands. It might kill people. If the goal of the regime is to maintain power, choosing among these options can be very difficult. For example, violence might quell a revolution, or it might foment more of it. In Hong Kong, the Chinese government has faced exactly that dilemma. Violent suppression of the protests might prove counterproductive.

It is important to emphasize that successful movements are not simply about the *revelation* of preferences, experiences, beliefs, and values. They are also about the transformation of preferences, beliefs, and values—most obviously on the part of perpetrators (those who engage in bad acts), but equally relevantly on the part of victims. Any social movement helps to change preferences, beliefs, and values. It casts a new light on past experiences. It does not merely elicit preexisting judgments; it produces fresh ones. Many social movements are intended to turn embarrassment and shame into a sense of dignity.

Recall the statement from a computer programmer from Syria: "When you meet somebody coming out of Syria for the first time, you start to hear the same sentences. That everything is okay. . . . It'll take him like six months, up to one year, to become a normal human being, to say what he thinks, what he feels. Then they might start . . . whispering. They won't speak loudly."

But eventually they might.

FOUR

Lapidation and Apology

This is not a sermon, not exactly, but let us begin with a passage from the Gospel according to John:

> Jesus went unto the mount of Olives.
> And early in the morning he came again into the temple, and all the people came unto him; and he sat down, and taught them.
> And the scribes and Pharisees brought unto him a woman taken in adultery; and when they had set her in the midst,
> They say unto him, Master, this woman was taken in adultery, in the very act.
> Now Moses in the law commanded us, that such should be stoned: but what sayest thou?
> This they said, tempting him, that they might have to accuse him. But Jesus stooped down, and with his finger wrote on the ground, as though he heard them not.
> So when they continued asking him, he lifted up himself, and said unto them, He that is without sin among you, let him first cast a stone at her.

And again he stooped down, and wrote on the ground.
And they which heard it, being convicted by their own conscience, went out one by one, beginning at the eldest, even unto
the last: and Jesus was left alone, and the woman standing in
the midst.
When Jesus had lifted up himself, and saw none but the woman,
he said unto her, Woman, where are those thine accusers? hath
no man condemned thee?
She said, No man, Lord. And Jesus said unto her, Neither do I
condemn thee: go, and sin no more.[1]

The English language needs a word for what happens when a
group of people, outraged by a real or imagined transgression,
responds in a way that is disproportionate to the occasion, ruining the transgressor's day, month, year, or life. I propose that we
repurpose an old word: *lapidation*.[2] Technically, the word is a
synonym for stoning, but it sounds less violent. That is a major
advantage, because as I understand it here, lapidation is not literally violent. It might provoke threats or even include threats, but
it is not actual stoning. The term is also obscure, which is again
an advantage; its obscurity makes it easier to enlist it for contemporary purposes.

Transgressions

To see what I have in mind, consider some examples:

1. Ronald Sullivan is a Harvard law professor who joined the
   team of lawyers defending Hollywood producer Harvey
   Weinstein against charges of rape and sexual abuse. A
   group of students rallied and protested against him,

attacked his character, and called for his removal as faculty dean at Winthrop House. Their call succeeded. Harvard ended Sullivan's deanship.[3]

2. Noah Carl is a young sociologist who was awarded a fellowship at Cambridge University's St Edmund's College. Carl has published research on trust and intelligence in well-regarded journals. He has also written shorter, less formal papers involving immigration and racial differences that some readers found offensive. A Cambridge professor of mathematics wrote a letter in protest of Carl's appointment demanding a formal investigation. Eventually hundreds of faculty and students signed that letter. An investigation was undertaken, and Carl was asked to leave St Edmund's.[4]

3. Representative Ilhan Omar made some statements, provocative or perhaps worse, about Israel and its American supporters. The comments provoked a flood of outrage.[5] She ultimately received numerous death threats.[6]

4. At various points in her career, Senator Elizabeth Warren has claimed that she has Native American ancestry. Those claims affected her candidacy for presidency, in part because President Donald Trump referred to her as "Pocahontas."[7]

5. In 2017, former Senator Al Franken was accused of having engaged in sexually aggressive behavior, including unwanted touching. He was essentially forced to resign from the U.S. Senate.[8]

Each of these cases can be seen to involve lapidation as I am understanding it here. In the most extreme situations, lapidation is based on a lie, a mistake, or a misunderstanding. People are lapidated even though they did nothing wrong. They might have made some misstatement that was misinterpreted by reasonable listeners. Even so, they did not intend to say what they were heard to say.

In less extreme cases, the transgression is real, and lapidators have a legitimate concern. They are right to complain and to emphasize that people have been saddened, hurt, or wronged. The problem is that they lose a sense of proportion. They want heads to roll. Someone makes a mistake or utters a foolish or offensive comment, and lapidators come out in force, often in a state of frenzy. Usually they are led by *lapidation entrepreneurs*, who have their own agenda. They might be concerned with self-promotion. They might be concerned with promoting a cause or with defeating an opponent, for whom the lapidation victim is taken to stand or can be made to stand. They may want to make the occasion for lapidation stand for the opponent, so that the opponent, or the cause for which he or she stands, *is* that occasion. ("He is Spartacus," more or less.) Lapidation entrepreneurs may unleash something horrific. That might be intentional.

We can ask hard questions about the precise definition. If there is a small burst of outrage on campus or on social media, ought we to speak of lapidation? If people receive threats in the mail, have they been lapidated? The best answer is that while some cases are de minimis, a matter of trivial concern, lapidation can occur even when participation is low and the outcry is not exactly loud. Even if a few stones are thrown, people might get hurt.

A more fundamental question: can lapidation be justified? Simply as defined here, it cannot be. No one should doubt that groups of people offended or outraged by statements or actions can be entirely right. What they seek, and what they do, may not be disproportionate. We might therefore have hard cases in which reasonable people dispute whether lapidation has happened. The disagreement is about the merits—about whether an explosion of outrage is warranted or not. No one should doubt that in some cases, outrage is warranted. It would be good to have a term for warranted outrage. By definition here, lapidation is not that term. It is reserved for excessive or unjustified reactions.

In ancient times, people were stoned for adultery and idolatry.[9] This is a clue to what triggers the practice. Like its old namesake, contemporary lapidation typically occurs when a person or institution *has violated a taboo*. Lapidators operate as a kind of private police force, enforcing some intensely held moral or political commitment that they believe to be at risk. Lapidators want to affirm, strengthen, or impose the taboo on certain words or deeds. They want to establish what is not normal, in the sense of being beyond the pale. The intensity of their reaction, and their effort to enlist large numbers of people in their enterprise, testifies to that fact.

Because the focus is on violations of taboos, we can understand why lapidation comes in so many shapes and sizes, and why it helps signal a kind of tribal identity. Left-of-center lapidators typically point to what they see as racist, sexist, and homophobic behavior. #MeToo is a case in point. To be sure, much of the #MeToo movement was justified and hence does not count as lapidation at all; consider the case of Harvey Weinstein, who was charged not only with sexual harassment but also with rape. Other cases are much less clear. My point is that lapidation follows from a particular set of substantive commitments and taboos that follow from those commitments.

Right-of-center lapidators tend to focus on what they see as disloyalty, disrespect for authority, lack of patriotism, or hypocrisy (a particular favorite, for especially interesting reasons). In his work on moral foundations, Jonathan Haidt contends that conservatives place far greater emphasis than liberals on authority, loyalty, and purity.[10] Haidt's work illuminates the distinctly right-of-center nature of some kinds of lapidation. When someone suggests some kind of disloyalty, particularly to the nation itself, right-wing lapidators tend to come out in force.

Group Polarization

What makes lapidation possible? Much of the answer is provided by the process of *group polarization*, which means that when like-minded people speak with one another, they tend to go to extremes.[11] In this phenomenon, members of a deliberating group typically end up in a more extreme position in line with their inclinations before deliberation began. Group polarization is the usual pattern with deliberating groups. It has been found in hundreds of studies involving more than a dozen countries, including the United States, France, and Germany.

It follows that a group of people who think that immigration is a serious problem will, after discussion, think that immigration is a horribly serious problem; that those who dislike the Affordable Care Act will think, after discussion, that the Affordable Care Act is truly awful; that those who approve of an ongoing war effort will, as a result of discussion, become still more enthusiastic about that effort; that people who dislike a nation's leaders will dislike those leaders quite intensely after talking with one another; and that people who disapprove of the United States and are suspicious of its intentions will increase their disapproval and suspicion if they exchange points of view. (There is specific evidence of the latter phenomenon among citizens of France.)[12] When like-minded people talk with one another, they usually end up embracing a more extreme version of the position to which the average member was inclined before they started to talk. It should be readily apparent that enclaves of people inclined to rebellion or even violence might move sharply in that direction as a consequence of internal deliberations. Political extremism is often a product of group polarization.

Suppose people begin with the thought that Ronald Sullivan probably ought not to have agreed to represent Harvey Weinstein, or that Al Franken did something pretty bad. If so, their discussions will probably make them more unified and more confident about those beliefs, and ultimately more extreme. A key reason involves the dynamics of outrage.[13] Whenever some trans-gression has occurred, people want to appear at least as appalled as others in their social group. That can transform mere disap-proval into lapidation.

Expressivism

Why do people lapidate? Consider this claim from Sandra Cason, a protestor in the 1960s: "If I had known that not a single lunch counter would open as a result of my action I could not have done differently than I did. If I had known violence would result, I could not have done differently than I did. I am thankful for the sit-ins if for no other reason than that they provided me with an opportunity for making a slogan into a reality, by turning a decision into an action. It seems to me that this is what life is all about."[14]

This is a claim about the *expressive* nature of some political action. It captures something important about lapidation—a sense that consequences are irrelevant. Note Cason's proud sug-gestion that she "could not have" acted differently even if her actions were futile, and even if her actions led to violence and were in that sense perverse.

Many behavioral scientists distinguish between two families of cognitive operations in the human mind: System 1, which is fast, automatic, and intuitive, and System 2, which is slow, calcu-lative, and deliberative.[15] When people recognize a smiling face, add 2 plus 2, or know how to get to their bathroom in the middle of the night, System 1 is at work. When they first learn to drive or multiply 563 times 322, people must rely on System 2.

System 1 is distinctly associated with identifiable behavioral biases. People often show "present bias," focusing on the short term and downplaying the future.[16] For better or for worse, most people tend to be unrealistically optimistic.[17] In assessing risks, people use heuristics, or mental shortcuts, that often work well but sometimes lead them in unfortunate directions. With respect to probability, people's intuitions go badly wrong, in the sense that they produce serious, even life-threatening mistakes. Lapidation is typically a matter of System 1—a quick, automatic reaction to a real or perceived transgression.

Compare Sandra Cason's words with Herbert Simon's: "We are all Expressionists part of the time. Sometimes we just want to scream loudly at injustice, or to stand up and be counted. These are noble motives, but any serious revolutionist must often deprive himself of the pleasures of self-expression. He must judge his actions by their ultimate effects on institutions."[18]

Lapidation is often expressive, not based on a judgment about its effects on institutions. When people lapidate, they may think that they are achieving something important. Maybe they are; maybe they are not. They may succeed in ruining a reputation or forcing a resignation. When their cause is just, that may be justified and important, even essential. But if social change is the goal, the immense amount of time and emotional energy expended on lapidation would often be better spent elsewhere.

Apologies

For its victims, lapidation can be a living nightmare. Some receive death threats. Even when their security is not at risk, they carry a stamp of shame from which they may never fully recover. Too often, that is a grievous wrong. What should they do? A tempting answer is simple: they should apologize. Put to one side the moral question and assume that their goal is solely strategic: to make it stop. Is an apology a good idea?

It might be. An apology might give the lapidators a sense that they have won. At least this is so if the apology is taken as not merely an admission of wrongdoing but also as a kind of self-abasement, a way of begging for forgiveness.[19] Lapidators might think: We have achieved what we wanted to achieve. Now let us move on.

But there is another possibility. Lapidators might smell blood. They might think that they have received the equivalent of a confession, which means that lapidation will continue until there is some kind of execution (a retreat from public life, a forced resignation, a criminal prosecution, a criminal conviction). Everything depends on the distribution of emotions and beliefs among lapidators—how merciful and focused they are inclined to be.

There is not a great deal of empirical work on this topic, but some evidence suggests that this admittedly vague account is broadly correct, and that apologies will often fail. Using Amazon Mechanical Turk, Richard Hanania conducted an experiment in which respondents were given two versions of real-life events in which public figures made controversial statements (and were lapidated).[20] In one version, the offender apologized; in the other, he did not. The first event involved Senator Rand Paul, who seemed to suggest that the Civil Rights Act of 1964 was wrong to forbid private discrimination on the basis of race. The second involved Lawrence Summers, who as president of Harvard University offered some provocative statements about why there were so few women scientists and engineers, pointing (among other things) to the possibility of inherent gender differences.

For example:

Version 1 (Apologetic):
In response, Rand Paul quickly took an apologetic tone and backtracked, saying he would never repeal the Civil Rights Act. In the years since, observers argue that he has been bending over backwards to make up for his original statements, particularly through minority outreach. He now says he does not question any aspect of the Civil Rights Act. Paul won his Senate seat, and still serves to this day.

Version 2 (Non-apologetic):
In the days after the controversy, Paul refused to explicitly apologize for his statements. He went on the offensive, claiming that his opponents were engaging in unfair political attacks. In response to one interviewer, he said, "What is going on here is an attempt to vilify us for partisan reasons. Where do your talking points come from?" Paul won his Senate seat, and still serves to this day.

After respondents were shown one or the other version of the story, they were initially asked: "How offensive did you find Paul's comments when reading about them?" They were also asked whether the controversy made them less likely to vote for Paul. For Summers, the experiment was similar, except respondents were asked, "Should Summers have faced negative consequences for his statements?"

For Paul, the apology had no effect in aggregate. For liberals, the apology appeared to have a negative effect, but it fell short of significance. For Summers, the apology turned out to have a (significant) negative effect in aggregate. Disaggregating across groups in the Summers case, the negative effect was especially large among women and liberals; there was no significant effect one way or the other among men, conservatives, or moderates. For both Summers and Paul, the effect of an apology was to make women more supportive of punishment, but there was no effect on men. *No* group, in either case, was less inclined to punish the offender as a result of an apology.

It is not clear how to generalize these findings. Suppose a politician offends political conservatives by saying (for example) that the United States is a force for evil in the world and should own up to its misdeeds; that those who want to regulate abortion believe in male supremacy and are seeking to preserve it; that hunting should be banned; or that no white person can possibly understand what it is like to be African American. After an apology, we might imagine something like the mirror image of the findings just described: perhaps conservatives would seek more punishment while liberals would be unmoved. Or perhaps an apology would have a beneficial effect, leading people, on average, to be less inclined to favor punishment. For some of these imagined comments, whites and men might be more inclined to punishment after hearing an apology, whereas African Americans and women might be less inclined—or even more angered by the apology than they were by the original remarks.

To obtain further perspective on these questions, I conducted a survey on Amazon Mechanical Turk, presenting four scenarios to four groups of four hundred people. As in Hanania's study, the sample was not nationally representative, but each group of four hundred was demographically diverse and contained people from different political parties. We can see my survey as a kind of pilot, supporting Hanania's basic findings, and thus adding to a body of work suggesting that in certain circumstances, apologies by public figures may not help and might even hurt. I presented a brisk scenario to the participants of each group, ending with the question: "Would you be more inclined to support a public official, less so, or neither?" in each case.

1. Suppose that a recent nominee for the position of secretary of state said, a few years ago, "I think the United States should apologize for the many terrible things that it has done in the world." Suppose that the comment has caused a great deal of controversy. If the nominee said, "I apologize for that statement; it was foolish of me to say that," would you be . . .
2. Suppose that a presidential candidate said, a few years ago, "People who want to ban abortion just don't care

about women." Suppose that the comment has caused a great deal of controversy. If the candidate said, "I apologize for that statement; it was foolish of me to say that," would you be . . .

3. Suppose that a presidential candidate has been accused, by a number of women, of inappropriate touching—of getting too close to them, of hugging them too much, of hugging them too long. Some of the women have said, "I felt violated." If the candidate said, "I apologize for what I did; it was not right, and I will cease and desist," would you be . . .

4. Suppose that a nominee for the position of attorney general said, a few years ago, "Gays and lesbians are violating God's will. Marriage should be between Adam and Eve, not Adam and Steve." Suppose that the comments have become controversial. If the nominee said, "I apologize for that statement; it was offensive, hurtful, and wrong," would you be . . .

For all four questions, the general tendency was for people to become less rather than more inclined to support a political figure after an apology. For the first question, 41.5 percent said they would be less inclined to support; 23 percent said they would be more inclined; 35.5 percent said neither. For the second question, 36.5 percent were less inclined to support; 19.95 percent were more inclined; 43.55 percent were neither. The corresponding numbers for the third question were 29.38 percent less inclined, 24.94 percent more inclined, 45.68 percent neither; and for the fourth, 36.84 percent less inclined, 21.8 percent more inclined, and 41.35 percent neither.

In every case, an apology tended to decrease rather than increase support for people who said or did offensive things. To be sure, there were interesting differences across political lines. For the first question, Democrats were far more likely to be less inclined to support (50.29 percent more likely versus 17.71 percent less likely), whereas Republicans were equally divided (33/32), and independents were in the middle (37.19/23.97). For the second question, apologies made both Democrats and independents less inclined rather than more inclined to support (42.35/17.87 for Democrats, 43/15 for Republicans), whereas Republicans were more inclined to support (24 percent less inclined, 32 percent more inclined). For the third question, both Democrats and Republicans were equally likely to become less inclined or more inclined to support but, puzzlingly, independents were more inclined to support (42/22). For the fourth question, Democrats (33/26.9), independents (41.5/13.3), and Republicans (36.5/24) were *all* inclined to be less supportive.

The differences here are intriguing, but the general lesson is clear. Across the relevant populations, apologies did not make people more inclined to support wrongdoers. To be sure, they did affect significant numbers of people in a positive way, and a great deal remains to be learned. We could certainly devise scenarios in which an apology would move the most relevant group in a positive direction. But to date, we have little evidence for the proposition that apologies in general decrease the opprobrium directed at real or imagined wrongdoers.

Freedom of Speech

Is lapidation protected by the First Amendment? To answer that question, we need to know some details. In my view, the constitutional issue deserves extended attention, with an emphasis on the inadequacies of existing constitutional law.[21] For now, some general points will have to suffice.

There is no lapidation exception to the First Amendment. A vehement, ugly, but truthful attack on a public official or private citizen will almost certainly receive constitutional protection.[22] Sarcasm and satire are certainly protected, and even if the line is crossed to hatred and rage, those too enjoy protection.[23] It follows that under existing doctrine, a central question—usually *the* central question—is whether the lapidation contains falsehoods. If so, it might be defamatory and thus regulable under the current constitutional standards, which sharply distinguish between public and private figures.[24] Under the familiar test: for public figures, a lapidator might be held liable if he or she knew that what was said was false, or if the person acted with reckless indifference to the question of truth or falsity.[25]

There is also a question of whether some forms of lapidation might count as "fighting words," long understood as a category of constitutionally unprotected speech.[26] Fighting words are statements that would induce a reasonable person to respond with physical force. By definition, lapidation consists of personal attacks, and even if they do not contain falsehoods, they might amount to a form of bullying, a kind of speech that might not be seen to deserve constitutional protection.[27] Here, it might seem, is an opportunity for constitutional restrictions on the most extreme forms of lapidation. On the other hand, the exclusion of fighting words from constitutional protection occurred before the post-1960 flowering of free speech doctrine, and it is not clear whether the idea of fighting words has any place in the context of falsehood-free attacks on public figures. The best conclusion might be that such figures must respond with their own words, not by invoking the courts.[28] If lapidation is generally protected by the First Amendment, notwithstanding the harm it causes, there is all the more reason for private institutions, including social media providers, to reduce or even stop it, including under the rubric of preventing bullying.[29]

There is a broader point in the background. Free speech law also emphasizes the problems with the "heckler's veto": if people despise speech and are trying to stop it, the obligation of the public authorities is to silence the heckler, not the speaker.[30] From the standpoint of free expression, a society that is prone to lapidation creates serious problems for itself.

The problems are most obvious, of course, when lapidation actually occurs. But anticipated lapidation also compromises free speech. If people know they will be lapidated, they will silence themselves. In some cases, of course, self-censorship can be a desirable check on offensive or harmful words. White supremacists might decline to say what they think because of the prospect of lapidation. No one should lament that. Norms of civility and decency serve essential functions, and they might be enforced by lapidators. But at the system level, it is hard to celebrate a situation in which the prospect of lapidation is causing people to silence themselves about their deepest convictions. There are complicated trade-offs to be made here.

We should not lapidate lapidators. But we might remind them of the words of a great opponent of lapidation: "He that is without sin among you, let him first cast a stone."

Founding

To many modern readers, *The Federalist* seems formal, musty, old, and a bit tired—a little like a national holiday, celebrating events long past but lacking a sense of struggle or even a clear message.[1] But its authors, Alexander Hamilton, James Madison, and John Jay, writing under the collective name "Publius" just a few years after the American Revolution, produced by far the best historical record of the ideas that gave birth to the American republic.

It is important and true that their essays were a product of a concrete historical drama involving the fate of an emerging nation that was having an exceedingly difficult time governing itself. But Publius's claims, and the political structure he defended, bear not only on American debates of the eighteenth century but also on those of the nineteenth, twentieth, and twenty-first. They offer lessons for making war and peace, and for domestic challenges of many different kinds. Indeed, they provide guidance for constitutional democracies all over the globe, not least when peace, prosperity, public health, and self-government itself are endangered.

In a nutshell, Publius contends that republican governments do best, and are most stable and most protective of liberty, not in a small, homogeneous area but in a large, diverse one, complete with a robust system of checks and balances. According to *The Federalist*, small republics and tightly knit groups often end up destroying liberty, and themselves, because of the power of well-organized factions.

But in a large republic, heterogeneity can be a creative force, promoting circumspection and introducing safeguards against bias, error, confusion, and oppression. In Madison's boldest words, the constitutional design, offering checks and balances in a large republic, provides "a Republican remedy for the diseases most incident to Republican government. And according to the degree of pleasure and pride we feel in being Republicans, ought to be our zeal in cherishing the spirit, and supporting the character of Federalists." Those words are bold because republicanism and federalism were widely thought to be opposed. (We will see why.)

Publius argues on behalf of a distinctive and novel kind of democracy—a deliberative one. He insists that in a well-functioning deliberative democracy, a wide range of perspectives and diversity of views are a virtue rather than a vice, at least if the constitutional framework has the correct structure. In this way,

Publius explicitly repudiates classical republicanism and Montesquieu, the great theorist of republican thought and an important authority for postrevolutionary America.

The repudiation yielded something altogether new. That novel conception of republicanism—one that cherishes the spirit of federalists—provides a clue to the longevity of the United States Constitution. It also helps explain why it has served, for so many, as a model of self-government under law. It helps explain, finally, why it has operated as a robust set of safeguards against (full-scale) authoritarianism.

A Republican Revolution

Many people think of the American Revolution as relatively conservative, as revolutions go. The French Revolution shook the world, and so did the Russian Revolution. The American version seems much milder. Maybe it was a matter of escaping British rule, but without fundamental changes in people's understandings of society and politics. After all, much of American law and culture, including our Constitution, draws directly on our British heritage. Americans refer proudly to Anglo-American traditions. Long before the Constitution, there was the Magna Carta. Were the British really so bad? Sure, the Americans didn't want to be ruled by a king, and no taxation without representation and all that, and we had some kind of tea party in Boston—but was there such a big break?

Yes, there was. In the decades that preceded the revolution, republicanism was on the rise, and it was a radical creed. As the

American colonists saw it, republicanism entailed self-government; their objection to British rule was founded on that principle. Republicanism takes many forms, and it can be traced all the way back to Rome. But the colonists were particularly influenced by the French theorist Montesquieu, who famously divided governments into three kinds: "A republican government is that in which the body, or only a part of the people, is possessed of the supreme power; monarchy, that in which a single person governs by fixed and established laws; a despotic government, that in which a single person directs everything by his own will and caprice."[2]

The colonies came to despise both monarchy and despotism. They thought that the former often led to the latter. The Declaration of Independence objects that "a long train of abuses and usurpations" from the monarchy "evinces a design to reduce" the colonies "under absolute Despotism." This objection led to the conclusion that "it is their right, it is their duty, to throw off such Government, and to provide new Guards for their future security."

In the colonies, republican thinking, focused on the supreme power of the people, led to fresh ideas about what governments can legitimately do. More broadly, it spurred new understandings of how human beings should relate to one another, and in the process undid many kinds of established hierarchies. The best and most vivid account comes from the historian Gordon Wood, who shows that the American Revolution was social as well as political, and that it involved an explosive principle: the

equal dignity of human beings.[3] In the early decades of the eighteenth century, Americans lived in a traditional society defined by
established hierarchies, which affected people's daily lives, their
beliefs, and their self-understandings. Wood writes that "common people" were "made to recognize and feel their subordina-
tion to gentlemen" so that those "in lowly stations . . . developed
what was called a 'down look.'" They "knew their place and willingly walked while gentlefolk rode; and as yet they seldom expressed any burning desire to change places with their betters."[4]
In Wood's account, it is impossible to "comprehend the distinc-
tiveness of that premodern world until we appreciate the extent
to which many ordinary people *still accepted their own lowliness.*"[5]
That acceptance had a political incarnation. In England, national
sovereignty was found in the king, and the king's American subjects humbly accepted that understanding.

As late as 1760, the colonies consisted of fewer than 2 million
people, subjects of the monarchy, living in economically under-
developed communities, isolated from the rest of the world.
They "still took for granted that society was and ought to be a
hierarchy of ranks and degrees of dependency."[6] Over the next
twenty years, their world was turned upside down, as the monarchical view of the world crumbled. The American Revolution
was a revolution of everyday values as well as politics. In Wood's
words, it was "as radical and social as any revolution in history,"
producing "a new society, unlike any that had ever existed any-
where in the world."[7]

It was republicanism, with its proud commitment to liberty

and equality, that obliterated the premodern world. Its transformative power could be felt everywhere, including in England itself. As David Hume put it, "To talk of a *king* as God's vice-regent on earth or to give him any of these magnificent titles which formerly dazzled mankind, would but excite laughter in everyone."[8] But the authority of republican thinking was especially pronounced in the American colonies. As the Revolution gathered steam, people were not laughing. Rule by the king wasn't funny. In 1776, Thomas Paine described the king as a "royal brute" and a "wretch" who had "the pretended title of Father of His People."[9]

David Ramsay, one of the nation's first historians (and himself captured by the British during the Revolution), marveled that Americans were transformed "from subjects to citizens." That was an "immense" difference because citizens "possess sovereignty. Subjects look up to a master, but citizens are so far equal, that none have hereditary rights superior to others."[10] As the transformation began, the practice of impeachment, which originated in England but had fallen into disuse there, started to take on a whole new meaning. It became Americanized. It turned into an instrument of popular sovereignty, an emphatically republican weapon in a place where the people might rule.

The thinking behind the Revolution led, of course, to an attack on royalty and aristocracy, and if republicanism was about anything, it was about that. But the same thinking placed a new focus on the aspirations, needs, and authority of ordinary people. Hierarchies of all kinds were bound to disintegrate—not through anything like envy but through the simple assertion, immortalized in the Declaration of Independence, that all men are created equal. As Wood puts it, "To focus, as we are today apt to do, on what the Revolution did not accomplish—highlighting and lamenting its failure to abolish slavery and change fundamentally the lot of women—is to miss the great significance of what it did accomplish: indeed, the Revolution made possible the antislavery and women's rights movements of the nineteenth century and in fact all our current egalitarian thinking."[11]

In the nineteenth century, Walt Whitman, America's poet laureate, spoke for the Revolution when he wrote, "Of Equality— as if it harm'd me, giving others the same chances and rights as myself—as if it were not indispensable to my own rights that others possess the same."[12] Bob Dylan, Whitman's successor, put it more simply:

> But even the President of the United States
> Sometimes must have
> To stand naked.[13]

The Articles of Confederation

To appreciate *The Federalist*, it is indispensable to have some understanding of the Articles of Confederation, which the Constitution replaced. The Articles were adopted shortly after the Revolution to ensure a degree of unification of the states, allowing them to address common foreign and domestic problems, but the overriding understanding was that the states remained sovereign. The first substantive provision of the Articles announced that "each state retains its sovereignty, freedom, and independence, and every Power, Jurisdiction, and right, which is not by this confederation expressly delegated to the United States, in Congress assembled."

A number of powers were, however, conferred on "the United States in Congress assembled." These included "the sole and exclusive right and power of determining on peace and war"; the authority to resolve disputes between the states; the power to regulate "the alloy and value of coin struck by their own authority, or by that of the respective states"; and the authority to control dealings with Indian tribes, to establish or regulate post offices, and to appoint naval and other offices in federal service.

By contemporary standards, the Articles of Confederation had conspicuous gaps. Two of the most important powers of the modern national government were missing altogether: the power to tax and the power to regulate commerce. Moreover, two of the three branches of the national government were entirely absent. There was no executive authority. There was no general national judicial authority; the only relevant provision authorized Congress to establish a national appellate tribunal to decide maritime cases. There was also no bill of rights.

By the middle years of the 1780s, many prominent leaders agreed that the Articles needed amendment. James Madison, along with many others, identified a series of concrete problems: encroachments by the states on federal authority, trespasses by some states on others, unjust state laws, and a disastrous absence of mechanisms for coordinated action in domains such as naturalization, commerce, and literary property. Seeking to address those problems, reformers agreed that a prime imperative was to prevent any form of authoritarianism, especially as they had experienced it under British rule, and thus to carry forward the goals for which the Revolution had been fought.

In 1786, state representatives met in Annapolis to discuss the problems that had arisen under the Articles; they adopted a resolution to hold a convention in Philadelphia to remedy those problems. The resulting Constitution developed an altogether novel framework that went beyond the Articles of Confederation in crucial ways.

Among the most important changes were the creation of a powerful executive branch; the grant to Congress of the powers to tax and to regulate commerce; and the creation of a federal judiciary, including the Supreme Court and, if Congress chose, lower federal courts. The Tenth Amendment, added two years later, was a pale echo of the first provision of the Articles of Confederation, deleting the word *expressly*, and it was countered by the clause granting Congress the authority to make "all laws necessary and proper" to effectuate its enumerated powers. To both its defenders and its critics, the most noteworthy feature of the new Constitution was the dramatic expansion in the authority of the national government, giving it a range of fresh powers and authorizing both the executive and the judiciary to exercise considerable authority over the citizenry.

The Constitution was sent to the states for ratification in September 1787. It proved extremely controversial. Powerful objections were offered, and there was no assurance that it would be ratified. Opposition was especially intense in New York. Seeking to persuade voters there, Alexander Hamilton decided to publish a series of essays in the *New York Packet*, the *Advertiser*, and other publications during late 1787 and early 1788; he recruited John Jay and James Madison for the effort. Because Jay was injured in a street riot at an early stage, he was able to contribute only two essays. The name Publius was chosen by Hamilton.

The Anti-Federalist Case

In many periods in American history, there has been enthusiasm for the arguments of the Anti-Federalists—committed opponents of the proposed Constitution who claimed that it amounted to a betrayal of the Revolution's principles. We cannot understand Publius's originality without exploring the relationship between his arguments and those of the Anti-Federalists.

Many Anti-Federalists emphasized the importance, for republican government, of civic virtue. Governmental outcomes were, in their view, to be determined by citizens devoted to a public good separate from the struggle of private interests; and one of government's key tasks was to ensure the flourishing of the necessary public-spiritedness. In part for this reason, the Anti-Federalists assigned great importance to decentralization. Only in small communities was it possible to check a potentially oppressive government and to find and develop the unselfishness and devotion to the public good on which genuine freedom depends.

In emphasizing the value of small communities, the Anti-

Federalists echoed traditional republican theory. Consider the words of Montesquieu, a crucial authority for Anti-Federalists and federalists alike: "In a large republic, the public good is sacrificed to a thousand views; it is subordinate to exceptions, and depends on accidents. In a small one, the interest of the public is easier perceived, better understood, and more within the reach of every citizen; abuses are of less extent, and of course are less protected."[14]

Emphasizing this point, the Anti-Federalists were deeply hostile to a dramatic expansion in the powers of the national government. Only a decentralized society would allow the homogeneity and dedication to the public good that would prevent the government from threatening liberty and degenerating into a war among private interests. A powerful national government would create heterogeneity and distance from the sphere of power—and thereby both threaten liberty and undermine the public's willingness to participate in politics as citizens.

The Anti-Federalist Brutus, a close follower of Montesquieu, was most explicit on the importance of homogeneity: "In a republic, the manners, sentiments, and interests of the people should be similar. If this be not the case, there will be a constant clashing of opinions; and the representatives of one part will be continually striving against those of the other. This will retard the operations of government, and prevent such conclusions as will promote the public good."[15] Many of the Anti-Federalists also sought to avoid extreme disparities in wealth, education, or power. Such disparities would poison the spirit of civic virtue and prevent the homogeneity of a virtuous people. The Anti-Federalists complained of "the factitious appearances of grandeur and wealth."[16]

From this perspective, the grounds on which the Anti-Federalists based their opposition to the proposed Constitution should be clear. They believed that the Constitution would destroy the decentralization on which true liberty depended. Citizens would lose effective control over their representatives. Rule by remote national leaders would attenuate the scheme of representation, rupturing the alliance of interests between the rulers and the ruled. The Anti-Federalists feared that the proposed Constitution would exclude the people from the realm of public affairs and give weakly accountable national leaders enormous discretion to make policy and law.

Some of the Anti-Federalists were also skeptical of the emerging interest in commercial development that had played such a prominent role in the decision to abandon the Articles of Confederation. In the Anti-Federalists' view, commerce threatened the principles underlying the Revolution because it gave rise to ambition, avarice, and the dissolution of communal bonds.

Publius's Response

The Anti-Federalist objections to the proposed Constitution provoked Publius to offer a response that amounted to a new conception of self-government. This conception revised long-standing principles of republicanism and rejected some of its apparently deepest commitments.

The authors of *The Federalist* were fully aware of how original the American project was. No. 1, written by Hamilton, begins in this way: "It has been frequently remarked that it seems to have been reserved to the people of this country, by their conduct and example, to decide the important question, whether societies of men are really capable or not of establishing good government from reflection and choice, or whether they are forever destined to depend for their political constitutions on accident and force." What is especially noteworthy here is the distinction between "reflection and choice" on the one hand and "accident and force" on the other, with the suggestion that many constitutions were a product either of random events or of simple power. Suggesting that cherished and time-honored traditions might actually be a product of "accident and force," Publius proposed a fresh path.

But how might the apparently powerful objections of the Anti-Federalists be shown to be unconvincing? It is best to start with Madison's No. 10, probably the greatest of the papers. For Madison, the primary problem for self-government is the control of faction, understood in his famous formulation as "a number of citizens, whether amounting to a majority or minority of the whole, who are united and actuated by some common impulse of passion, or of interest, adverse to the rights of other citizens, or to the permanent and aggregate interests of the community." Madison urges that for a well-constructed union, no advantage "deserves to be more accurately developed than its tendency to break and control the violence of faction."

Note Madison's emphasis on both passion and interest—and his suggestion that either one can harm "the rights of other citizens" to "the permanent and aggregate interests of the community." We can see Nazi Germany and the Soviet Union as animated more by passion than interest; the same is true of many nations that have stifled liberty. But interest also plays a role, as when nations confiscate property or when majorities harm minorities whom they see as competitors. The horrific internment of Japanese Americans during World War II was a product of passion, but it was partly based on perceived interest.

In standard republican fashion, the Anti-Federalists rooted the problem of faction in that of corruption; their solution was to control the factional spirit by limiting the power of national representatives. In their view, those close to the people, chosen locally, would not stray from the people's interests. The civic virtue of the citizenry and of its representatives would guard against tyranny. In emphasizing the importance of small republics, the need for civic virtue, the risk of corruption, and the importance of homogeneity, the Anti-Federalists directly followed Montesquieu.

Madison saw things differently. Rather than focus on corruption, he emphasized the problem of faction, which he saw as fundamental. The "corruption" that created factions was, in his view, a natural though undesirable product of liberty and inequality in human faculties. This redefinition meant that the basic problems of governance could not be solved by the traditional republican means of education and inculcation of virtue.

To be sure, education and virtue were profoundly important. But they could not root out faction, which was built into the human condition.

Crucially, the problem of faction was likely to be most, not least, severe in a small republic. In a small republic, a self-interested private group could easily seize political power and distribute wealth or opportunities in its favor. In the view of the federalists, this is precisely what had happened in the years since the Revolution. Factions had usurped the processes of state government, putting both liberty and property at risk.

Madison viewed the nation's recent history as sufficient evidence that sound governance could not rely on traditional conceptions of civic virtue and public education to guard against factional tyranny. Such devices would be unable to overcome the natural self-interest of men and women, even in their capacity as political actors. "The latent causes of faction are thus sown in the nature of man." Self-interest, in Madison's view, would inevitably result from differences in natural talents and property ownership. To this point, Madison added the familiar idea that attempting to overcome self-interest would carry a risk of tyranny of its own.

Madison's Solution

All this justified Madison's rejection of the Anti-Federalist belief that the problem of faction could be overcome, but it supplied no positive solution. Madison's proposed solution was particularly original. He began with the notion that the problem posed by factions is especially acute in a small area, for a "common passion or interest will, in almost every case, be felt by a majority of the whole"—and minorities would have no protection. Liberty and self-government would be at risk. But in a large republic, the diversity of interests would ensure against the possibility that sufficient numbers of people would feel a common desire to oppress minorities.

A large republic thus contained a built-in check against factional tyranny. "The smaller the society, the fewer probably will be the distinct parties and interests composing it." But "extend the sphere, and you take in a greater variety of parties and interests; you make it less probable that a majority of the whole will have a common motive to invade the rights of other citizens." An extended republic, with diverse interests, creates strong protection against oppression.

This was not the only virtue of size. In a large republic, the principle of representation might substantially solve the problem of faction. In a critical passage, Madison wrote that representation would "refine and enlarge the public views by passing them through the medium of a chosen body of citizens, whose wisdom may best discern the true interest of their country and whose patriotism and love of justice will be least likely to sacrifice it to temporary or partial considerations." A large republic would also reduce the danger that representatives would acquire undue attachment to local interests. Emphasizing that risk, Madison favored large rather than small election districts and long rather than short periods of service. This conception of representation appears throughout *The Federalist*. No. 57 argues: "The aim of every political constitution is, or ought to be, first to obtain for rulers men who possess most wisdom to discern, and most virtue to pursue the common good of the society; and in the next place, to take the most effectual precautions for keeping them virtuous whilst they continue to hold their public trust."

In several places, Publius suggests that wisdom and virtue would characterize national representatives. Whereas the Anti-Federalists accepted representation as a necessary evil, Publius saw it as an opportunity for achieving governance by diverse officials devoted to a public good distinct from the struggle of private interests. The hope was for a genuinely national politics, in which representatives would have the time and temperament for reflection, discussion, and debate, from which the common good would emerge.

All this was sufficient to suggest that the standard view, rooted in Montesquieu and underlined by Brutus, was altogether wrong: small republics were far less promising guardians of self-government than large ones. But what about the risk of "clashing opinions," a problem that could only be greatly increased in a large republic? Here, Publius offers one of his most important arguments. The central claim is that what Brutus sees as a vice is actually a virtue.

In No. 70, Hamilton writes, "The differences of opinion, and the jarrings of parties in [the legislative] department of the government, though they may sometimes obstruct salutary plans, yet promote deliberation and circumspection, and serve to check excesses in the majority." Publius views the system of bicameralism as a way of ensuring increased "deliberation and circumspection," because it enlists diversity both as a safeguard and as a way of enlarging the range of arguments.

In the very same number, Hamilton actually defends the "unitary executive"—the decision to create a single president, who would be in charge of the executive branch and thus in a position to ensure "promptitude of decision" as well as energy. The unitary executive, in key ways subordinate to the legislature, was a crucial part of the system of deliberative democracy. As Hamilton explains in No. 79, an independent judiciary was also a crucial element: "The complete independence of the courts of justice is peculiarly essential in a limited constitution." A central function of the independent judiciary would be to interpret the Constitution and thus to ensure that the other institutions were kept within the bounds lawfully established by We the People.

In important respects, the departure from traditional republicanism could not have been greater. In Publius's account, the Constitution willingly abandoned the classical republican understanding that most citizens should participate directly in the processes of government. Far from being a threat to freedom, a large republic could help guarantee it. And in No. 55, Publius explicitly rejects the notion that political actions are inevitably vicious or self-interested: "As there is a degree of depravity in mankind which requires a certain degree of circumspection and distrust, so there are other qualities in human nature which justify a certain portion of esteem and confidence."

A Deliberative Democracy

Of course, representation was hardly the whole story. The structural provisions of the Constitution were designed to increase the likelihood of public-spirited representation, to provide safeguards in its absence, and to ensure an important measure of popular control.

Bicameralism was meant not only to promote "the jarrings of parties" but also to ensure that some representatives would be relatively isolated while others were relatively close to the people. Indirect election of representatives played a far more important role at the time of ratification than it does today; the fact that state legislatures chose senators ensured that one house of the national legislature would have additional insulation from political pressure. The Electoral College, puzzling to many modern observers, is another important example of the general effort to promote deliberation among those with different perspectives (see No. 68).

Perhaps most important, the separation of powers was designed with the recognition that even national representatives may be influenced by "interests" that are inconsistent with the public welfare. In No. 10, Madison notes that "enlightened statesmen will not always be at the helm." No. 51 elaborates this point with a distinctive emphasis, relying on the celebrated "policy of supplying, by opposite and rival interests, the defect of better motives." Whereas conventional republicans emphasized virtue, Madison offered a different prescription: ambition, in the classic formulation, "must be made to counteract ambition." He continued: "The interest of the man must be connected with the constitutional rights of the place. It may be a reflection on human nature, that such devices should be necessary to control the abuses of government. But what is government itself, but the greatest of all reflections on human nature? If men were angels, no government would be necessary. If angels were to govern men, neither external nor internal controls on government would be necessary. In framing a government which is to be administered by men over men, the great difficulty lies in this: you must first enable the government to control the governed; and in the next place oblige it to control itself."

Checks and balances within the federal structure were intended to constrain both self-interested representation and factional tyranny. If a private group achieved dominance over one part of the national government, or if a segment of rulers had interests that diverged from those of the people, other national officials would have both the incentive and the means to resist.

The federal system was another important safeguard. The "different governments will control each other" and ensure stalemate rather than action at the behest of particular private interests. The jealousy of state governments and the attachment of the citizenry to local interests would provide additional protection against the aggrandizement of power in national institutions.

The result is a complex system of checks. National representation, bicameralism, indirect election, distribution of powers, and the federal-state relationship would operate in concert to counteract the effects of faction despite the inevitability of the factional spirit. And the Constitution itself, enforced by independent judges and adopted in a moment when the factional spirit had been perhaps temporarily extinguished, would prevent both majorities and minorities from usurping government power to distribute wealth or opportunities in their favor.

The picture that emerges is one of deliberative democracy. Publius rejects the view of his Anti-Federalist adversaries on the ground that they missed the lessons of both theory and experience. They undervalued the likelihood that local government would be dominated by private interests; they were too optimistic in thinking that those interests could be subordinated by instilling principles of civic virtue. Finally, Publius thinks that commercial development is crucial to the new nation and cannot be achieved without considerable centralization.

The idea that politics is solely a process of bargaining and trade-offs was far from Publius's understanding. His suspicion of civic virtue, at least as a complete solution, and his skeptical attitude toward the possibility that citizens could escape their self-interest led him to reject the traditional republican structure, without rejecting important features of its understanding of politics. Hence Madison's stunning suggestion that the "pleasure and pride, we feel in being Republicans" does not lead to the doubts and fears of the Anti-Federalists, but instead to the Federalists' hope and optimism. Crucially, the system of checks and balances in a large republic would improve deliberation. In this system, judicial review was hardly a means of frustrating the public will; on the contrary, it would help ensure that We the People remain superior to our rulers.

Perhaps the most significant element in federalist thought was the expectation that the constitutional system would serve republican goals better than the traditional solution of small republics, civic education, and close ties between representatives and their publics. The federalists insisted that the new system of deliberative democracy would preserve the underlying republican model of politics without running the risk of tyranny or relying on naive beliefs about the human capacity to escape self-interest.

Was Publius Right?

Reasonable people have long wondered whether Publius was right. For a long time, the United States has been a beacon for people all over the globe, perhaps the clearest symbol of a system and a culture that stand opposed to authoritarianism in all its forms. But the national record is hardly spotless. For many decades, slavery was an accepted feature of the American system. In times of war, civil liberties and civil rights have been badly compromised—sometimes for sufficient reasons, sometimes not. Protection of freedom of speech is a product of the second half of the twentieth century; before that time, speech could be punished if it was regarded as dangerous. The system of checks and balances did not prevent legally mandated racial segregation.

This is not the place to offer a catalogue of abuses by the U.S. government or various states. But the fact that it is easy to produce one raises a cautionary note about any argument that Publius was entirely right. Anti-Federalist themes can be found in long-standing American skepticism about a centralized and sometimes remote national government—and in corresponding enthusiasm for the authority of state and local officials. Over the last decades, those themes have come mostly from political conservatives, in opposition to what many have seen as aggressive acts by Democratic leaders such as Lyndon Johnson, Bill Clinton, and Barack Obama. We may doubt whether those acts suggest a failure of Publius's project, but it is noteworthy that Anti-Federalist objections continue to play a role in American political debate.

At important times in American history, an independent judiciary has not been seen as a bulwark of liberty but as a threat to self-government, very much in line with the Anti-Federalists' fears. In the early part of the twentieth century, federal courts struck down progressive legislation, such as laws regulating maximum workday hours and mandating the minimum wage. Decades later, courts struck down laws prohibiting use of contraceptives and abortion, laws that discriminated by sex, and restrictions on voting rights. Decades after that, courts struck down campaign finance regulation, gun control laws, and affirmative action programs. No one can plausibly argue that an occasionally aggressive federal judiciary has brought authoritarianism to the United States. But Publius certainly did not anticipate it.

In a large republic, interest groups, or factions, have wielded considerable power, requiring serious qualifications of Madison's arguments in No. 10. Here too, it would be difficult to argue that he was fundamentally wrong, but the United States is in important respects far smaller than it once was, among other things because it is so easy to communicate and organize across geographical barriers that were once formidable. In some areas, factions can and do take over the government's apparatus. There is also the rise of polarization. Although Publius anticipated and embraced checks and balances, he did not foresee intense party identifications, often paralyzing the national legislature. The inability of Congress to deal with pressing national problems is partly a product of political polarization, making people unwilling to work with one another. That has been a serious problem.

But it may well be the rise of an immensely powerful presidency, alongside the growth of the national security and administrative apparatus, that has raised the most serious questions about Publius's claims. At the time of the founding, and notwithstanding the fear of monarchies, the legislature was widely seen as the most dangerous branch. Today it is often paralyzed, and when it is not, it tends to follow the president's lead.

Although Publius was greatly concerned to constrain the authority of the executive, he did not anticipate this situation. As he put it:

In a government where numerous and extensive prerogatives are placed in the hands of an hereditary monarch, the executive department is very justly regarded as the source of danger, and watched with all the jealousy which a zeal for liberty ought to inspire. In a democracy, where a multitude of people exercise in person the legislative functions, and are continually exposed, by their incapacity for regular deliberation and concerted measures, to the ambitious intrigues of their executive magistrates, tyranny may well be apprehended, on some favorable emergency, to start up in the same quarter. But in a representative republic, where the executive magistracy is carefully limited; both in the extent and the duration of its power; and where the legislative power is exercised by an assembly, which is inspired, by a supposed influence over the people, with an intrepid confidence in its own strength; which is sufficiently numerous to feel all the passions which actuate a multitude, yet not so numerous as to be incapable of pursuing the objects of its passions, by means which reason prescribes; it is against the enterprising ambition of this department that the people ought to indulge all their jealousy and exhaust all their precautions.

It is a subtle argument, but its modern force is doubtful. One reason is that in the twenty-first-century "representative republic" that is the United States, the executive magistracy is not so carefully limited in the extent and the duration of its power. Especially since the New Deal, presidents and those who work for them have wielded massive, awe-inspiring, occasionally fear-producing policy-making authority. It is a nice question whether Publius's claims about republican government remain convincing in light of the rise of an immensely powerful presidency.

What can constrain it, if it is really determined to move in authoritarian directions? Even centuries later, some of the central answers do come from Publius.

First: The system of checks and balances ensures, now as ever, that the president almost always needs legislative authorization in order to act. At least in the domestic domain, he cannot act unilaterally; Congress must give him the power to do what he wants. This is not a perfect guarantee. In theory, of course, a president can simply ignore that restriction on his authority. In practice, that could happen (and it has happened, for example, under President Abraham Lincoln and Franklin Delano Roosevelt, two of the nation's greatest presidents). But at least most of the time, it is not terribly likely. Publius was more focused on the dangers associated with Congress, but the design of the national government did serve to limit the president's room to maneuver, even under radically changed conditions. One more time, however: this is not a perfect guarantee.

Second: The federal judiciary is generally available to insist that the executive must obey the law. Most of the time, it acts as a deterrent to unlawful action and also as a corrective when such action occurs. When President Harry Truman seized the nation's steel mills in the midst of the Korean War, the Supreme Court struck down his action. When President Richard Nixon tried to prevent the publication of the Pentagon Papers, the Supreme Court stopped him. To be sure, the president appoints the nation's judges, and we can imagine a federal judiciary that is supine in the face of presidential aggression. We cannot rule out the possibility that that will happen. But imagination is one thing; reality is another. At least in general, the judiciary has been available to prevent or correct the worst abuses.

Third: The Bill of Rights has assumed far more importance than the founding generation expected. It is now a defining feature of American law and, equally important, American culture. Authoritarian measures are likely to run into serious objections under one or another provision of the Bill of Rights—protecting due process, the free exercise of religion, freedom of speech, the right to a jury trial. Likelihoods are no more than that, but it is important to have them on the right side.

Fourth: In the American republic, the court of public opinion often imposes severe constraints on what national officials do. Publius was well aware of this point. And because respect for rights and for the central ingredients of self-government are culturally ingrained, public opinion is a serious check on the executive—both on what it can do and on what it wants to do.

There is a cautionary note. Institutional safeguards can alter probabilities, but they ensure nothing. As we have seen, the system of checks and balances is far less robust than Publius expected, because legislatures generally support presidents of their political party—which means that ambition is less likely to counteract ambition. Some of the time, ambition reinforces ambition, as legislators bow (supinely) to the will of the chief executive. Under President Donald Trump, Republican members of Congress did not exactly insist on congressional prerogatives; almost all of the time, they did whatever Trump wanted.

In any case, Congress often gives broad authority to the executive branch, even in domestic policy, which means that the president can move national policy largely in the direction he wants. If the American project is to be seriously jeopardized, it might well be because of a very grave security threat, actual or perceived. And the success of President Trump has made many people fear that a president, with his current powers, might have the ability to undermine the foundations of a democratic order, above all by altering the understanding of what counts as normal.

It is true that the sheer longevity of our constitutional framework, and the place it has maintained for both democracy and deliberation, attest to the power of Publius's arguments. Much of that power consists in the establishment of bounds on what can and cannot be done—bounds that are a product of norms as well as law. Taken as a whole, the American experience suggests that Publius did not go far wrong. But nothing is foreordained.

SIX

Refounding

It is hard to amend the United States Constitution. Under Article V, an amendment can be proposed only with the approval of either two-thirds of both houses of Congress or the legislatures of two-thirds of the states. It is difficult enough to obtain that level of agreement, but there is another obstacle, which is that no proposed amendment can be ratified without agreement from either three-fourths of the state legislatures or conventions in three-fourths of the states. The authors of the Constitution knew exactly what they were doing. They wanted to limit amendments to what James Madison called "great and extraordinary occasions." After their successful revolution, they sought to normalize the republic they had created.

Their plan worked. In well over two centuries, only twenty-seven constitutional amendments have been ratified. Two periods of large-scale constitutional change stand out. In 1791, the nation added the ten amendments that constitute the Bill of Rights, thus rejecting Madison's view that an explicit enumeration of rights was unnecessary. After the Civil War, the nation added three amendments that (among other things) abolished slavery, applied the due process clause to state governments, adopted a new principle of "equal protection," and guaranteed African Americans the right to vote. The Civil War amendments were a radical departure from the original Constitution insofar as they attempted to eliminate slavery and its legacy and also created a new set of rights, enforceable against state governments. In the fullness of time, those rights would be understood to include essentially all of the original Bill of Rights, which had previously been applicable only to the national government. Because of the magnitude of those changes, we can in fact see the Civil War amendments as creating a new Constitution.

The Bill of Rights and the Civil War amendments account for nearly half of the total. Other amendments allow Congress to collect income taxes, call for direct elections of senators, forbid denial of the vote to women, impose a two-term limit on presidents, prohibit poll taxes, and allow all citizens who are eighteen or older to vote. In the successful efforts to amend the Constitution, a recurring theme has been improvement of self-government, above all by extending the right to vote.

As a member of the Supreme Court from 1975 to 2010, John Paul Stevens was widely liked and admired. Modest and eclectic, he could not be pigeonholed, and he displayed a consistent openness to both facts and arguments. He frequently emphasized that under the American Constitution, the government must be "impartial," and he exemplified impartiality with his capacity to listen, his unfailing humility, and his insistence on giving respectful attention to opposing views. Stevens also revered the American Constitution. Remarkably, at the age of ninety-four he published a book calling for no fewer than six amendments to the nation's founding document.[1] No Supreme Court justice, sitting or retired, had ever done anything like it.

It is noteworthy, though perhaps not surprising, that every one of Stevens's proposed amendments would overturn what he saw as a wrongheaded decision by the Supreme Court. He was a dissenter in each of these cases. It is also noteworthy that Stevens's broadest theme is the ideal of democratic self-rule. His general goal is to promote an ideal that, as he sees it, has been badly compromised by the Court. His concern is that majorities of the Supreme Court have established a new normal, and he hopes that We the People can restore what he believes to be the right balance.

Every one of those rulings could have gone the other way. Most were decided by 5–4 margins. Everything depended on which justice retired when, and which president was able to replace whom. Like political life, the arc of constitutional law is full of serendipity and contingency (a point to which I will return in chapter 10). To the extent that constitutional law can promote or compromise democracy, a lot turns on happenstance. Stevens's analysis provides a good occasion for discussing that point, and also for exploring amendments to the Constitution, which are a central way in which We the People exercise our ultimate authority.

Let's begin with gun control. The Second Amendment states: "A well regulated Militia, being necessary to the security of a free State, the right of the people to keep and bear Arms, shall not be infringed." For over two hundred years, federal courts interpreted the Second Amendment narrowly. In their view, the opening reference to a "well regulated Militia" limited the scope of the amendment. The Second Amendment did not create a freestanding individual right to have guns.

Well-organized groups, above all the National Rifle Association, rejected this interpretation and insisted that the Second Amendment did indeed create an individual right. For many years the NRA's view was widely regarded as ideology masquerading as constitutional law. Stevens notes that even as late as 1991, retired chief justice Warren Burger—a well-known conservative appointed by President Richard Nixon—said that the Second Amendment "has been the subject of one of the greatest pieces of fraud, I repeat the word 'fraud,' on the American public by special interest groups that I have ever seen in my lifetime."

It is remarkable but true that in 2008, in *District of Columbia* v. *Heller*, a majority of the Supreme Court accepted the very view that Burger considered a "fraud."[2] Stevens thinks that in so ruling, the Court departed from the original understanding of the Second Amendment, and in the process greatly increased judicial power to oversee what state and federal governments do to prevent gun violence. He laments that a constitutional provision, originally adopted to protect the federal government from interfering with the states' power to ensure that their militias were "well regulated," is now seen as giving federal judges the ultimate power to determine the validity of state regulations of both civilian and militia-related uses of arms.

Stevens thinks democratic processes, not federal judges, should decide the fate of regulations designed to minimize gun violence. As a remedy for "what every American can recognize as an ongoing national tragedy," he would amend the Second Amendment to specify that it applies only to those who keep and bear arms "when serving in the Militia." What is especially remarkable is that as late as 2000, that would have been unnecessary because the Constitution was widely understood to mean exactly that—and that by 2016, Stevens's proposal would seem radical because it would disrupt what had become, in both politics and law, the new normal.

Stevens begins his discussion of campaign finance with the Court's 2010 decision in the *Citizens United* case, which held that under the First Amendment, Congress cannot limit the ability of corporations to make independent expenditures on political campaigns.[3] In that case, Stevens wrote an eighty-six-page dissent, but his most fundamental objection is to a critical part of the Court's opinion in its first significant campaign finance case, *Buckley* v. *Valeo*.[4] At the time, the Court upheld restrictions on campaign *contributions*, ruling that such restrictions could provide legitimate protection against corrupt practices. (*Citizens United* did not disturb that ruling.) But it simultaneously struck down restrictions on campaign *expenditures*, which people spend on their own behalf and do not contribute to anyone. (Think, for example, of Michael Bloomberg's ill-fated but well-funded campaign for the presidency in 2020.) In a key passage, the Court said that "the concept that government may restrict the speech of some elements of our society in order to enhance the relative voice of others is wholly foreign to the First Amendment."

This conclusion was exceedingly important, because it meant that campaign finance limits could never be justified as a way of promoting political equality or ensuring that inequalities in wealth are not translated into inequalities in political power. Stevens believes that the Court made a big mistake here. To be sure, he agrees that speech about controversial issues "may not be censored for the purpose of enhancing the persuasive appeal of either side of the debate." But he thinks it is altogether different, and entirely legitimate, to restrict the quantity of speech in order to give "adversaries an equal opportunity to persuade a decision maker to reach one conclusion rather than another."

Acknowledging that some campaign finance limits may be too low, he insists that Congress should be able to act to reduce the risk that wealth will be the deciding factor in contested elections. Hence his proposed constitutional amendment, which would allow Congress and state governments to impose "reasonable limits on the amount of money that candidates for public office, or their supporters, may spend in election campaigns."

In 1972, the Supreme Court seemed to be on the verge of ruling that the death penalty is cruel and unusual punishment, prohibited by the Eighth Amendment.[5] But in 1976, the Court backed off, allowing the death penalty so long as its imposition was preceded by a set of procedural safeguards designed to reduce the risk that innocent people would be executed.[6] Stevens joined the majority at the time, and for most of his years on the Court he accepted that basic approach.

In 2008, however, he concluded that because the risk of executing the innocent could not be eliminated, the death penalty must be abolished. Here he insists that the ultimate penalty is unlikely to deter violent crime and that its real motive is retribution. In his view, that is not sufficient justification, because execution of innocent people is not "tolerable in a civilized society." He would amend the Constitution to entrench that judgment.

The Constitution is universally understood to forbid racial gerrymanders. No state can structure its electoral districts so that they all have majorities of white people. But political gerrymanders favoring one party are pervasive, and under existing law they are not going to be struck down; the Supreme Court has ruled that the legitimacy of political gerrymanders presents a "political question" not suited to judicial resolution.[7] Stevens thinks that from the standpoint of democratic self-government, this is a most unfortunate result, because it makes general elections far less competitive and ensures that in many places the primary elections are what matter. As a result, "Gerrymandering has made our elected officials more doctrinaire and less willing to compromise with members of the opposite party."

Stevens contends that political gerrymandering is responsible for a wide range of bad things and "may well have been the principal cause of the government shutdown that occurred in October 2013." He would amend the Constitution to say that districts "shall be compact and composed of contiguous territory" and that any departures from that requirement cannot be motivated by an "interest in enhancing or preserving the political power of the party in control of the state government."

Issues of federalism, as such, rarely get people's blood boiling, but Stevens is greatly troubled by a seemingly technical principle that constitutional lawyers know as the "anti-commandeering rule." The Court gave birth to that idea relatively recently. In 1997, it decided *Printz* v. *United States*, which prohibits Congress from requiring state officials to perform federal duties (hence the term "commandeering").[8] Congress had sought to require state law enforcement officers to make a "reasonable effort" to determine whether a proposed sale of a firearm would be lawful, but the Court ruled that under the Constitution, Congress must respect the sovereignty of state governments and cannot force state authorities to take the actions that it deems fit. Stevens insists that this idea is not merely wrong and inconsistent with the original constitutional plan but also dangerous, because it might turn out to damage "the federal government's ability to respond effectively to natural disasters that recur with distressing frequency." He would amend the Constitution to eliminate the anti-commandeering rule.

Sovereign immunity is an ancient English doctrine that states that the sovereign (meaning the government) cannot be sued without its consent. The idea is sometimes connected to the view that "the king can do no wrong." In Stevens's account, this doctrine is un-American. It had little appeal in the nation's first century, having been explicitly rejected by Chief Justice John Marshall and also by Abraham Lincoln, who said: "It is as much the duty of Government to render prompt justice against itself, in favor of its citizens, as it is to administer the same between private individuals."

After the Civil War, however, the Court began to construe the Constitution so as to create barriers to lawsuits brought by citizens against states as such. In recent decades, the Court has said that the Constitution does not allow Congress to give private parties the right to obtain damages against state treasuries when states have acted inconsistently with the Fair Labor Standards Act or denied people benefits payments in violation of federal law.

Stevens believes that the Court's decisions to immunize official wrongdoing have not only departed from the constitutional plan but produced serious unfairness. He believes that if a hospital is owned by a state, it should not have sovereign immunity when an otherwise identical hospital, owned privately, would have to pay damages. Because a congressional enactment would be struck down, he would amend the Constitution to deprive states of sovereign immunity for violating federal law.

Gun control, campaign finance, capital punishment, political gerrymandering, anti-commandeering, and sovereign immunity— it's a heterogeneous list. But there is a unifying theme, which is the importance of democratic self-government. Stevens believes that in too many domains, that ideal has been compromised, and he fears that we are taking the compromising for granted. With respect to gun control, campaign finance, anti-commandeering, and sovereign immunity, Stevens would free the political process from the control of the courts. In the case of political gerrymandering, he would go in the other direction, imposing a constitutional barrier where one does not now exist. But the reason for the barrier is to improve the functioning of American democracy. It is only in the case of the death penalty that Stevens would create a new rights-based safeguard designed to protect an individual right, not to promote self-government as such.

There is a general lesson here. A Republican appointee to the Supreme Court, having served for thirty-five years with mostly Republican appointees and under three Republican-appointed chief justices, argued for constitutional amendments that would largely entrench judicial restraint and reduce the role of the federal courts in American political life. His proposals attest to the fact that in recent decades, the most aggressive judicial decisions have tended to come from the Right—and to have an uncomfortable overlap with the political positions of the conservative wing of the Republican Party.

However much one may applaud or deplore that tendency, Stevens's book raises a more fundamental question: whether and when the Constitution should be amended to correct mistaken or harmful decisions by the Supreme Court. After all, those decisions tend to establish a new normal; in short order, people might get used to them, even if they were wrong. But no one thinks that whenever the Court errs, the nation should amend the Constitution to set things right. Do we have, in any or all of the six cases discussed here, a sufficiently "great and extraordinary occasion" to justify constitutional amendments? The answer depends in part on the burden that must be met by those who seek such amendments. Exactly how great, and how extraordinary?

Some people think that by making the Constitution so hard to amend, the founding generation compromised self-government, reducing the capacity of We the People to alter their handiwork. In principle, there is no abstract answer to the question of whether a constitution should be made easy or difficult to amend; we need details. If a nation's constitution is full of mistakes, or if its high court is systematically misinterpreting it, easy amendment might be a good idea. If we should adopt a strong presumption against constitutional change, it must be because the existing document is excellent, or at least excellent enough, so that frequent or easy amendments are likely to make things worse rather than better.

Throughout American history, citizens have maintained the equivalent of an arms control agreement, in which they practice mutual forbearance with respect to constitutional change. In previous decades, some people have vigorously supported amendments that would allow school prayer, make a commitment to gender equality, impose term limits on members of Congress, protect "victims' rights," allow states to ban same-sex marriages and flag burning, and require a balanced budget. None of these has been ratified.

You might think that the Constitution would be better if one or more of these amendments were part of it, but you might agree that the general pattern of forbearance is also in the national interest. You might even think that the founding generation was wise to make forbearance more likely, if only because of the importance of constitutional stability and the risk of harmful or ill-considered amendments. There could well be strong national majorities in favor of some amendments that Justice Stevens and civil libertarians would deplore, while national majorities would be exceedingly difficult to muster for some of the amendments he proposes—a point that might strengthen the case for forbearance. And if you approve of forbearance, you might be inclined to reject most or all of Stevens's proposals even if you think he is mostly right on what policy makes best sense.

Consider the two federalism issues, anti-commandeering and sovereign immunity. Stevens is correct to suggest that if Congress deems it necessary to require state officials to take certain actions—say, to combat a natural disaster—it is hard to see why the Constitution should stand in its way. And if states have violated federal law, and injured people in the process, the national legislature should be authorized to require them to pay compensation. By their very design, the compositions of the Senate and the House of Representatives make it unlikely that Congress will be inattentive to the legitimate concerns of states as such.

But in both cases, we might wonder whether the problems are serious enough to call for constitutional change. If the federal government cannot commandeer the states, it might be able to persuade them to help voluntarily, or to act either on its own or with the private sector to achieve its goals. As the law now stands, principles of sovereign immunity generally do not bar people from suing states to require them to comply with federal law. The main function of sovereign immunity is to prevent people from invading state treasuries to obtain monetary damages. That's unfair, to be sure, but is it really a "great and extraordinary occasion" justifying a change to our founding document?

On gun control, there is some reason to think that constitutional change is unwarranted, which Stevens himself emphasizes: at least as of now, the Court's rulings continue to leave considerable flexibility to state and federal governments. True, the Court has recognized an individual right to bear arms, but it has pointedly declined to impose anything like an across-the-board barrier to gun control. The individual right remains relatively narrow, and if states or the nation really want to impose new limits on gun ownership, they can do a great deal.

The Obama administration, for example, proposed a number of new restrictions, including background checks for all gun sales, a ban on military-style assault weapons, and a limitation on magazines to a capacity of ten rounds. These restrictions, and many more, would be fully consistent with the Second Amendment as the Supreme Court understands it. The principal obstacle to new gun control legislation is an absence of political will, not the Second Amendment. And in light of the strong political opposition to any such legislation, it is an understatement to say that a constitutional amendment would be extremely difficult to obtain.

With respect to capital punishment, any judgment will, of course, depend on contested questions of both fact and value. Stevens is right to say that no legal system containing the death penalty can fully eliminate the risk of executing innocent people. One recent study estimates that over 4 percent of all death row inmates were wrongly convicted. If you consider the risk of executing the innocent to be intolerable, or if you believe that capital punishment is an unconscionable barbarity, you will very probably support his proposal.

Moreover, Stevens has a good argument that political gerrymandering is creating serious problems for our system of self-government, above all because it allows political parties to entrench themselves and also contributes to a high degree of polarization in Washington. Stevens is also convincing with respect to campaign finance regulation. In the defining First Amendment cases—many of which involve restrictions on speech during wartime—the political majority is attempting to entrench itself by censoring speech that it deems to be dangerous. The free speech principle forbids that kind of self-entrenchment. It ensures political liberty and, with respect to ideas, a kind of political equality. But the purpose of campaign finance regulation is not to entrench the power or opinions of the majority but to ensure that economic inequalities are not turned into political ones. In a society that tolerates disparities in wealth, that is not merely a worthy goal; it is essential. As those disparities continue or even grow, there is a serious risk that wealthy people will be able to buy not only their preferred goods and services, as they are certainly entitled to do, but also their preferred policies and candidates, which is anathema to a system that prizes self-government.

To be sure, some campaign finance restrictions could turn out to protect incumbents. But the best way to combat that risk is through democratic debate, not through judicially imposed constraints on campaign finance laws as such. In support of his proposed amendment, Stevens could invoke the views of James Madison, who was not at all enthusiastic about economic equality, but who insisted on the importance of "establishing a political equality among all." In the end, Madison himself might be willing to agree that in the twenty-first century, a democratic effort to promote that ideal would count as a "great and extraordinary occasion."

SEVEN

Radicals

What is radicalism really about? When does it make sense? Do we need it now? An effective way to change norms, and the conception of what is normal, is for small groups of people—and possibly for just one person—to cast doubt on widespread beliefs and assumptions. For better or worse, radicals often serve that function.

I am going to explore efforts to revise norms in radical ways through the lens of *Young Radicals*, a superb book by Jeremy Mc-Carter, who depicts the lives and views of five American radicals who thought that society had to be remade in fundamental ways.[1] Their views resonate today. McCarter's cast of characters—John Reed, Alice Paul, Randolph Bourne, Max Eastman, and Walter Lippmann—includes five enduring radical "types": Manicheans, democrats, identitarians, propagandists, and technocrats. (It might seem odd to classify technocrats as "radicals," but as we shall see, it makes sense to do that; they might even deserve pride of place.) All of these types should be immediately recognizable, especially on the political left, though we can find analogues on the right as well.

I will suggest, with some qualifications, that contemporary democracies do not need Manicheans, propagandists, and iden-titarians. (I will be especially hard on the first and last of these.) But we do need democrats, at least of a certain kind. Insofar as she opposed something like a caste system, Alice Paul was an American hero. We also need technocrats, whom we will not be able to categorize in ideological terms. Democracies, I will argue, can and should be technocratic.

The Manichean

Was there ever a writer like John Reed? Swashbuckling, mischievous, exuberant, and vain, he was both insufferable and difficult to resist. Here's how McCarter introduces him: "John Reed prowls the docks, laughing with the sailors, chatting up the whores."

Walter Lippmann knew Reed well, and in an affectionate, merciless profile titled "Legendary John Reed," he ridiculed Reed's initial attempts to embrace socialism: "He made an effort to believe that the working class is not composed of miners, plumbers, and working men generally, but is a fine, statuesque giant who stands on a high hill facing the sun." Disdaining one of the most celebrated young journalists of the time, Lippmann proclaimed that "by temperament he is not a professional writer or reporter. He is a person who enjoys himself. Revolution, literature, poetry, they are only things which hold him at times, incidents merely of his living. . . . I can't think of a form of disaster which John Reed hasn't tried and enjoyed." But he also offered a tribute: "Wherever his sympathies marched with the facts, Reed was superb."[2]

Reed began his career as a poet as well as a journalist, making his reputation with jubilant, silly, memorable verses about Greenwich Village and its bohemians: "O Life is a joy to a broth of a boy / At Forty-Two Washington Square!" He offered his own merciless portrait of Lippmann:

> Our all-unchallenged Chief! But were there one
> Who builds a world, and leaves out all the fun,—
> Who dreams a pageant, gorgeous, infinite,
> And then leaves all the color out of it,—
> Who wants to make the human race, and me,
> March to a geometric Q.E.D.—
> Who but must laugh, if such a man there be?
> Who would not weep, if Walter L. were he?[3]

As McCarter puts it, Reed became, for various radicals and dissidents, "part crown prince, part jester," and much of McCarter's book can be read as a tale of the pitched battle between Reed, perpetually young, and that "all-unchallenged Chief," middle-aged before his time. But Reed also had a serious streak. He was a Manichean, because the struggle between good and evil excited him and gave his life a kind of meaning. Eastman, editor of the socialist magazine *The Masses*, ran Reed's stories and made him part of the journal's small, informal editorial board. To-gether, they wrote the magazine's manifesto, which sounds like Reed's self-understanding: "A revolutionary and not a reform magazine; a magazine with a sense of humor and no respect for the respectable; frank, arrogant, impertinent, searching for the true causes; a magazine directed against rigidity and dogma wher-ever it is found; printing what is too naked or true for a money-making press; a magazine whose final policy is to do as it pleases and conciliate nobody, not even its readers—there is a field for this publication in America."

While writing for *The Masses*, Reed created scenes, literally and figuratively. With radical friends and workers, he master-minded the performance of a play on Fifth Avenue. Displaying a picket line, the shooting of a striker, and the resulting funeral procession, the play received national publicity. He had an affair with his patron, the wealthy heiress Mabel Dodge, who fell des-perately in love with him. He became a war correspondent, push-ing his way to the middle of the Mexican Revolution, where he danced, drank, and sang with the rebels who followed Pancho Villa. When war broke out in Europe, he headed straight to Paris, "frantic to reach the front lines." He returned to Green-wich Village more sincerely radical; he now saw war as a "capi-talist swindle." After Lippmann endorsed Theodore Roosevelt for president, Reed broke savagely with his old friend, accusing him of having betrayed his radical principles and of supporting a monster. He broke up with Dodge and fell in love with Louise Bryant, a married writer.

When the United States entered World War I, Reed was devastated. He wrote numerous essays for *The Masses* attacking both
the logic and the justice of U.S. engagement. In 1917 he found
his way to Russia, having been told that "the new world was
being born there." There he met Leon Trotsky, who dazzled him,
explaining that the soviets (councils of workers, peasants, and
soldiers) are "the most perfect representatives of the people—
perfect in their revolutionary experience, in their ideas and objects." Reed was entranced. He covered the Russian Revolution,
eventually producing his classic, *Ten Days That Shook the World*
(1919). He hoped for a revolution in the United States in which
"the proletariat will finally lose its temper and rise" and "blood
will flow—in rivers." No longer a dilettante, he became a genuine revolutionary, probably the most important Communist in
the United States. As editor of the *New York Communist*, he got
to know Lenin. He was prepared to take orders directly from
Moscow, where the Bolsheviks created the Third Communist International, an organization that steered what they hoped would
be the global revolution. Reed died of typhus in 1920, with Bryant holding his hand. In Moscow, he received a hero's funeral.
He is buried at the Kremlin.

The Democrat

Alice Paul grew up in a traditional Quaker family whose members sometimes addressed each other as "thou," but she embraced
highly advanced ideas about gender equality and a commitment
to making the world a better place. At a young age, she joined the

National American Woman Suffrage Association and, working on her own, she effectively served as its congressional committee. On the eve of President Woodrow Wilson's inauguration in 1913, she organized a monumental suffrage parade in the nation's capital. Two weeks later, she found herself in the White House face-to-face with the new president, who emphasized that his priorities were currency reform and tariff reform. "But, Mr. President," Paul asked, "do you not understand that the Administration has no right to legislate for currency, tariff, and any other reform without first getting the consent of women to these reforms?" Wilson's baffled response: "Get the consent of women?"

Paul became a thorn in Wilson's side. Relentless, optimistic, inventive, and laser-focused, she started a magazine—the *Suffragist*—and founded the Congressional Union for Woman Suffrage, whose purpose was to raise funds to fight to amend the Constitution. Later she created the National Woman's Party in order to bring political pressure to bear on those who did not support the suffrage amendment. As the war began, she redoubled her efforts, proclaiming: "We have no true democracy in this country, even though we are fighting for democracy abroad. Twenty million American citizens are denied a voice in their own government. We must let the public know that this intolerable situation exists because, toward women, President Wilson has adopted the attitude of an autocratic ruler."

Her message got through to her fellow citizens. (Eastman, Bourne, and Reed endorsed her efforts.) With a huge crowd watching, two women unfurled a banner as Russian diplomats entered the White House gates: "We, the Women of America, tell you that America is not a democracy." Paul was arrested for unlawful picketing and put in jail, where she faced horrendous conditions. "The food is vile beyond belief, consisting of worm-ridden pork, bug-ridden soup, and stale bread." She refused to eat and was moved to the prison's psychiatric ward. In what can only be described as a form of torture, she was forcibly fed raw eggs through a tube. Her life was in danger, but she was suddenly released—possibly through personal intervention by the president.

Wilson eventually came around and publicly supported the suffrage amendment. To the nation and Congress, he spoke very much as Paul had a few years before, arguing that the suffrage movement is a test of whether "we be indeed democrats, and wish to lead the world to democracy." The House of Representatives voted for the amendment, but the Senate was unmoved.

Paul did not think that Wilson's commitment was firm enough. In 1919 she arranged to have him burned in effigy, right outside the White House. In June, Congress voted in favor of the amendment, and in 1920, the states ratified the Nineteenth Amendment to the Constitution. For the next fifty years, Paul served as leader of the National Woman's Party, which worked to ratify the Equal Rights Amendment, of which she was the original author back in 1923. She did not succeed. But at the age of seventy-nine, she played a key role in getting the Civil Rights Act of 1964 to forbid discrimination on the basis of sex. That ban continues to have a major impact on American life and is now essentially uncontested.

The Identitarian

Born with a facial deformity and a hunchback, and just five feet tall, Randolph Bourne was a theorist of identity. In 1911, he wrote an unusual essay called "The Handicapped," part of which was deeply personal:

> When one . . . is in full possession of his faculties, and can move about freely, bearing simply a crooked back and an unsightly face, he is perforce drawn into all the currents of life. Particularly if he has his own way in the world to make, his road is apt to be hard and rugged, and he will penetrate to an unusual depth in his interpretation both of the world's attitude toward such misfortunes, and of the attitude toward the world which such misfortunes tend to cultivate in men like him. For he has all the battles of a stronger man to fight, and he is at a double disadvantage in fighting them. . . . He is never confident of himself, because he has grown up in an atmosphere where nobody has been very confident of him; and yet his environment and circumstances call out all sorts of ambitions and energies in him which, from the nature of his case, are bound to be immediately thwarted.

His most influential essay was published in 1916. Titled "Trans-National America," it celebrates the dismal failure of the American idea of the "melting pot." With a few details tweaked, it could have been written this year. In Bourne's view, the failure of the melting pot, "far from closing the great American democratic experiment, means that it has only just begun." America, he wrote, was becoming "not a nationality but a trans-nationality, a weaving back and forth, with the other lands, of many threads of all sizes and colors."

With these ideas, Bourne was able to give new meaning to an idea of the American philosopher Josiah Royce: the "Beloved Community," in which people would retain their individual identities even as they expressed loyalty to their community. For Bourne, that ideal did not involve celebration of "mere doubtful triumphs of the past, which redound to the glory of only one of our transnationalities." (Consider a triumph that could be seen to involve only white men.) It would instead require a "future America, on which all can unite," created as those who are different come to "understand each other more warmly."

Bourne was also a vigorous opponent of American participation in World War I, and he lost his job at the *New Republic* because of his beliefs. In subsequent essays, relegated to journals with a much smaller readership, he deplored what he saw as his friends' and colleagues' betrayal of their shared ideals. "To those of us who still retain an irreconcilable animus against war, it has been a bitter experience to see the unanimity with which the American intellectuals have thrown their support to the use of war-technique in the crisis in which America found herself." Here are some of his most characteristic thoughts: "The intellectual who retains his animus against war will push out more boldly than ever to make his case solid against it. The old ideals crumble; new ideals must be forged. His mind will continue to roam widely and ceaselessly. The thing he will fear most is premature crystallization. If the American intellectual class rivets itself to a 'liberal' philosophy that perpetuates the old errors, there will then be need for 'democrats' whose task will be to divide, confuse, disturb, keep the intellectual waters constantly in motion to prevent any such ice from ever forming."

Bourne was always skeptical of "premature crystallization"— skepticism that was linked, I believe, to his rejection of the idea of the melting pot, which also involved an erasure of differences and a kind of crystallization, and which struck him as static and deadening. He wanted to recognize and respect differences. He died during the pandemic of 1918.

The Propagandist

Max Eastman made his reputation as editor of *The Masses*, a position that he accepted reluctantly in 1912, when he was just twenty-nine years old. The magazine was effectively dead at the time; it was tedious and broke. But Eastman transformed it, making it funnier and bolder. He put color on the cover. He added fiction, satire, and poetry. He devoted the middle two pages of one issue to an illustration portraying the New York press as a whorehouse, in which a rich man, labeled "Big Advertisers," has access to the prostitutes, "who are really the men working at a newspaper in incongruously silky dresses." Eastman's most important substantive decision was his refusal to choose between the pragmatic socialists like Lippmann, who wanted to win elections, and more extreme radicals who accepted the use of violence to combat capitalism. He made space for both positions.

Eastman's changes rescued the magazine. A glimpse of his own writing: "The world can be significantly divided into those who are always glad when a convict escapes, and those who are always sorry—with a small remnant who use judgment about individual cases. I don't use judgment about individual cases. I'm always glad." (So Eastman was a Manichean as well.) More earnestly: "Another thing about the Income Tax is that it really offers a method by which a great big redistribution of wealth could be effected, if the right people got the power. By the right people I mean the revolutionary workers and their allies who have the courage to fight for a Great Big Redistribution."

Like Bourne, Eastman vigorously opposed the war and, along with Reed, he repeatedly railed against it in *The Masses*. Eastman eventually faced serious criminal charges as a result of wartime legislation that made it a crime to obstruct recruitment for military service. He was brought to trial, but thanks to a hung jury, he narrowly avoided jail. Ultimately, free speech did not prevail. As a result of the Espionage Act of 1917, *The Masses* had to close down.

Eastman helped found another radical magazine, the *Liberator*. Like Reed, he became enraptured by what he saw as the success of the Russian Revolution—and lost his moorings. Despite having been a target of censorship himself, he seemed to embrace tyranny: "The most rigid political tyranny conceivable, if it accompanied the elimination of wage-slavery and continued to produce wealth, would increase the amount of actual liberty so much that the very sides of the earth would heave with relief."

Perhaps informed by his own experience, he argued, "So long as our civilization consists in its economic essence of a war between two classes, Free Speech will exist only at such times, or to such extent as may be harmless to the interests of the class in power." A lifelong poet, he still wanted "to cultivate the poetry, but keep the poetry true to the science of the revolution." (Good luck with that.)

Eastman decided to leave the United States to spend two years in Russia, to see (by his own account) whether what he had been writing was actually true. He did not like Stalin, and over the coming decades came to repudiate his previous thinking, describing socialism as "a dangerous fairy tale." In the 1940s, he became a friend and admirer of Friedrich Hayek, socialism's greatest critic. In the early 1950s, he supported Joseph McCarthy.

The Technocrat

Though Walter Lippmann began as a radical, he became an establishment figure, perhaps the most respected journalist in the United States, wined and dined by the nation's leaders, including several presidents. In his early twenties, he embraced socialism. Later he cofounded the *New Republic*, which rapidly became highly influential. Before the 1916 election, Woodrow Wilson himself courted Lippmann—and charmed him. "I have come around completely to Wilson," Lippmann told a friend, and in October he endorsed him publicly as "a constructive nationalist" whose purpose was "liberal in scope." He was invited to the White House.

When Wilson decided to join the war effort, Lippmann, who

supported that decision, reached out to his friend Newton Baker, the secretary of war, to seek employment with the War Department (in part, it appears, to avoid the draft). Baker obliged him. By all accounts, Lippmann did terrific work, impressing everyone, including many important figures in Washington. Even the famously skeptical Oliver Wendell Holmes Jr. proclaimed him a "monstrous clever lad." To Lippmann's delight, Wilson chose him for diplomatic work related to the peace conference that would follow the war.

As his old colleagues Bourne and Eastman rose in status in the antiwar camp—and became increasingly marginalized in the mainstream press—Lippmann's importance in the Wilson administration continued to grow. After leaving the government, he returned to journalism, won two Pulitzer Prizes, and served as an occasional adviser to several presidents. In 1964 he was awarded the Presidential Medal of Freedom. His work ranged over numerous topics and, to say the least, is not easy to pigeonhole. But let's bite the bullet: at his most original and interesting, Lippmann was a technocrat. In policy making, he wanted to carve out a larger role for experts, including scientists—people who actually knew what they were talking about. In an era in which he had been surrounded by radicals of very different kinds, emphasizing popular revolt, his plea for expertise in governance stood out.

Models of Radicalism

None of these figures was willing to rest content with what was normal. If we are looking for a new normal, should they inspire us today? Should we follow them? Or should we look for other models?

To answer these questions, we need to ask what their goals were and what they did to achieve them. Reed is an unforgettable character, and he produced some superb work, but what chiefly interested him was drama and bullets, not ideas, substance, or even people. He liked to divide the world into the good and the bad. It's hard to find kindness in his work. In a way, he was merciless. His radicalism ultimately took the form of an ardent embrace of Soviet-style Communism. That's not exactly admirable. Would he have embraced Hitler too? Probably not, but you can't rule it out. There is no question that the Nazis would have excited him. He lived for excitement. He wanted to burn down the house. He craved life, and he understood it as a kind of tumult, a battle of big "isms."

We can see John Reed in many young radicals, on the left and on the right, who find something large and historic to demonize (religion, the New Deal, statism, liberalism, modernity) and who are drawn above all to abstractions and transformational events, along with upheaval and destruction. A way to identify them: they hate what they hate more than they like what they like.

Bourne and Eastman certainly had strong moral commitments. Bourne was a man of deep feeling, and his life had great poignancy. He could easily become a hero to contemporary identitarians. (It is a bit of a puzzle that he hasn't.) He was unquestionably interesting. He was right to say that the metaphor of a melting pot is far too simple. But it does capture an idea: a shared national identity through which people of disparate racial, ethnic, and religious backgrounds come to identify as distinctively American. That is an admirable ideal. It makes a form of civic equality possible; it softens social divisions; it is often friendly and kind. It's not clear to what extent Bourne would repudiate that idea, or even what a "transnational America" really means.

Bourne was a precursor of the multiculturalists of the 1980s and 1990s, and of modern theorists and practitioners of identity politics. At their best, they capture people's actual experiences and their keen sense of exclusion and humiliation. That can be both helpful and important. Bourne sought to give people a sense of being recognized and of having some kind of home. He was making a plea, or a demand, for understanding and respect. That should not be diminished. With respect to government, the question is where, exactly, does it lead? We can identify potential answers: prohibitions on discrimination, affirmative action policies, perhaps reparations for African Americans, welcoming and even celebrating differences. But which differences, exactly? Eye color and foot size would be unlikely candidates. Bourne and his modern-day analogues focus on traditional sources of disadvantage and in particular on people of color, women, gays and lesbians, the disabled, and transgender persons.

In many domains, that focus has led in the right directions; it has certainly expanded the domain of the normal. Consider, for example, the requirements of the Americans with Disabilities Act, which call for "reasonable accommodation." Those requirements, leading to wheelchair access and more flexible work schedules, have certainly altered what people take to be normal, and in general, that is all to the good. As a large-scale approach to politics and law, however, a focus on "identity" has serious limitations. Consider the question of how to handle COVID-19, food safety, cigarette smoking, occupational safety, air pollution, or deaths on the highways. For so many of the questions on which governments must focus, identity is not the central issue (even if it might turn out to be relevant to important questions, including effectiveness and trust).

Eastman's work for *The Masses* displays wit and verve, and he produced a massive amount of both. But for all his passion, productivity, and sense of life, it's not unfair to wonder how much he contributed to either political theory or political practice. Propagandists can help causes and disseminate ideas, but it's reasonable to question whether they can leave much of a legacy. At their best they are translators, in the sense that they take ideas and give them currency. If the ideas are good ones, great. For the most part, Eastman's ideas were not good ones. Certainly that is true for his long embrace of socialism, which was defined more by generalized outrage than by policy prescriptions.

Paul and Lippmann are far more inspiring figures, and they are inspiring for altogether different reasons. Paul devoted much of her life to making American democracy live up to its own ideals. She opposed systematic exclusion. She hoped to expand and to contract people's conception of what was normal. She had a clear political vision—equality on the basis of gender—and for all her life, she stayed true to it. She was a radical about gender equality. She was relentlessly single-minded. She was right, and her views are now mainstream. Astonishingly, she changed the Constitution in a fundamental way, in the process making a massive mark on American law and life. There is a good argument that she belongs in an extended family with James Madison and Alexander Hamilton as one of the nation's founders.

For those who focus on how the United States falls short of democratic commitments, Paul provides a kind of compass. Those who speak for #MeToo, at its best, are following in her footsteps. If we want to generalize from what Paul did, we might suggest that she embraced a kind of anti-caste principle, maintaining that morally irrelevant characteristics (gender, race) should not be turned into systematic sources of social disadvantage. An anti-caste principle can claim deep roots in American theory and practice; it can be connected with the American Revolution itself, with its attack on the monarchical legacy and its insistence on the equal dignity of human beings. Of course, any anti-caste principle needs specification. But it is a promising start for any attack, old or new, on practices that entrench and perpetuate injustice. Too many people are suffering from such practices.

By contrast, Lippmann's most important work is a plea for a (heavily qualified) kind of technocracy. Lippmann was a democrat but a disaffected one, in the sense that the whole idea of self-government seemed to him misleading and simplistic. In his view, we need a stronger role for scientists and experts capable of overcoming the inevitable ignorance of the public. That was then, and is perhaps even more so now, an iconoclastic position. In some circles it is despised. But Lippmann's arguments deserve sustained attention. It is time, I think, for a Lippmann revival. Above all, his 1922 book *Public Opinion* repays careful reading.[4] It is clunky and labored, and no joy to read, but it is also astonishingly prescient.

Lippmann's thesis is that our conception of democracy is fundamentally flawed. In his view, we are asking voters and the press for something impossible: a fully accurate understanding of the world. The environment in which we live "is altogether too big, too complex, and too fleeting for direct acquaintance," and so "we have to reconstruct it on a simpler basis before we can manage with it." That simpler reconstruction is a "pseudo-environment," constructed in diverse ways by and for different groups, with the inevitable result that people end up living in "different worlds." More accurately, they live in the same world, but "think and feel in different ones." Pseudo-environments are by nature full of falsehoods and fake news. Opinions are manipulated, and consent is manufactured. (Think about climate change or the COVID-19 pandemic.)

Nor is the press a solution. "It is like the beam of a searchlight that moves restlessly about, bringing one episode and then another out of darkness into vision." In the end, people "are compelled to act without a reliable picture of the world," and this "is the primary defect of popular government, a defect inherent in its traditions."

In Lippmann's view, the last thing we need are earnest platitudes about governance by We the People. Of course the public is ultimately sovereign. But it needs to empower "a system of analysis and record"—that is, a government structure that makes space for statisticians, scientists, and other experts, who will acquire reliable information and make it accessible to both public officials and the public. Lippmann insists on a large role for technocrats, who are subject to representative government but who can disregard people's beliefs in various "pseudo-environments" and help public officials to deal with the world as it actually is. "The real sequence should be one where the disinterested expert first finds and formulates the facts for the man of action," with pride of place for the "experimental method in social science."

Expertise is "the way to overcome the central difficulty of self-government, the difficulty of dealing with an unseen reality." For those who worry about democratic ideals, Lippmann candidly insisted that his purpose "is not to burden every citizen with expert opinions on all questions, but to push the burden away from him towards the responsible administrator." (So Reed had Lippmann exactly right: "Who wants to make the human race, and me, / March to a geometric Q.E.D.") In its way, that is a radical thought. It shifts authority to people who specialize in particular domains. When he wrote, Lippmann was capturing an emerging trend in favor of administrative power conceived not as technocratic authoritarianism but as specific delegations to specialists, overseen by and accountable to democratic forces.

To be sure, no one ever marched under a banner bearing the words "responsible administration." But Lippmann was onto something important and too often neglected. We are used to thinking that large-scale questions legitimately split people with different political convictions, and that what separates citizens and nations are values, not facts. But think about air pollution, coronavirus, food safety, infrastructure reform, the opioid epidemic, increases in the minimum wage, and highway deaths. If we can agree on the facts, it should be possible to agree about what to do, or at least to narrow our disagreements.

We live in an era in which experts and technocrats are in disrepute. Obviously they can be arrogant or mistaken. They might act on the basis of their own values and interests, rather than their expertise. Facts alone cannot resolve hard questions about food safety, occupational health, pandemics, or climate change. But good technocrats are aware of their own fallibility; they have a duty to disclose what they do not know (and to stay in their lanes). It is important to ensure, through institutional design, transparency, and democratic accountability, that they are not empowered to act on the basis of private or ideological interests. All that is true and important. But we need expert help to fix a broken train, to deal with a serious medical problem, or to build a skyscraper. Many policy problems are similar. To deal with data privacy, health-care reform, infrastructure improvements, pandemics, and even climate change, we need specialists who can resolve difficult issues of fact.

Not all issues are like that, of course. We are unlikely to sort out moral disputes simply by clearing up the facts. If the question is the relationship between church and state or whether to allow abortion, empiricists cannot tell us everything we need to know. Alice Paul argued for democratic equality, not on behalf of demonstrable facts about men and women (though they might turn out to be relevant).

These are important qualifications. But what made Lippmann's argument noteworthy, and what gives it enduring appeal and contemporary urgency, is his emphasis on the centrality of the "responsible administrator" to public decision making— including when the most responsible form of administration is to rely, to a greater or lesser extent, on free markets. In the United States, and all over the world, there is far too much unnecessary suffering, often manifesting itself in premature death, mental illness, lack of opportunity, and chronic pain. We know enough to do a great deal about each of these.

That is not everything. But it is a lot. And as Lippmann said to his skeptics and colleagues—and to Eastman, Bourne, and above all Reed: "That is the radical way."

EIGHT

Liberalism

Do abstract ideas move history? Do "isms"? The answer cannot possibly be negative. Republicanism inspired the American Revolution as well as an assortment of social and cultural changes. Nazism, an unruly collection of abstract ideas, helped move a nation and in some respects the world. The same is true of Communism. Christianity has transformed not only individual lives but also morality and norms; among other things, it can be seen as a social movement, and it has decisively informed many other social movements.[1] Capitalism has promoted economic growth and affected social norms insofar as it insists on private property and freedom of contract.

These propositions themselves raise many questions. But we can acknowledge them while recognizing that most "isms" can be understood in dramatically different ways, and that they may be wide tents. (Nazism is an exception.) Republicanism can take many different forms, emphasizing, for example, populist or representative conceptions of self-government, and embracing radically different views about the separation of church and state. It is possible to endorse Communism, or at least the general idea, while having diverse views about freedom of speech, freedom of religion, democracy, and even property rights. Devout Christians embrace a wide assortment of positions on countless questions, political and otherwise, emphatically including the separation of church and state. Capitalism takes many forms, with a stronger or weaker commitment to some kind of welfare state. One cannot embrace capitalism while despising the idea of private property, but one can do so while abhorring or celebrating Franklin Delano Roosevelt's New Deal, the Endangered Species Act, or the Affordable Care Act.

In recent years, and with an apparent view to contemporary events, some people have mounted vigorous attacks on what they call "liberalism."[2] It is especially challenging to get traction on their claims because within the universe of "isms," liberalism includes a wide range of positions.[3] John Locke thought differently from Adam Smith, and John Rawls fundamentally disagreed with John Stuart Mill. Immanuel Kant, Benjamin Constant, Jeremy Bentham, Friedrich Hayek, Joseph Raz, Milton Friedman, Ronald Dworkin, and Jeremy Waldron are not easy to put in the same category. Some liberals, like Hayek and Friedman, emphasize the problems with centralized planning; other liberals, like Bentham and Raz, are not focused on that question at all. Isaiah Berlin, Jürgen Habermas, Robert Nozick, Susan Moller Okin, and Martha Nussbaum all count as liberals. Many of the great *practitioners* of liberalism—from James Madison and Alexander Hamilton to Abraham Lincoln to Franklin Delano Roosevelt to Martin Luther King Jr. to Margaret Thatcher and Ronald Reagan—did not commit themselves to foundational philosophical commitments of any kind (such as deontology or utilitarianism). This is so even if they were, in an important sense, political thinkers.

In these circumstances, any account of what liberalism "is" might amount to an argument in favor of one specification of liberalism rather than another. A strong candidate for the best account might begin with an insistence on the equal dignity of human beings, with an acknowledgment that equal dignity can be understood in different ways and grounded in different philosophical traditions.

There is also a complex and somewhat awkward relationship between liberalism as a philosophical position and liberalism as a political practice. The latter can be found in "neoliberalism," often understood as a call for economic liberty and respect for free markets. The European understanding of "liberalism" as a political creed is very different from the American understanding. In the United States, the term is often associated with left-of-center political positions, including (for example) insistence on gender equality, respect for same-sex marriage, movements for a "living wage," support for the Affordable Care Act, support for restrictions on certain forms of hate speech, claims for rigid separation of church and state, support for the Green New Deal, and openness to immigration. It is most unclear what these positions have to do with each other, at least as a matter of political philosophy. It is equally unclear whether they can be connected in any sense with the work of Locke, Kant, Mill, Bentham, Hayek, Raz, or Rawls.

But put these various claims to one side. Because of the diversity of views that can be found within the liberal tent, it is not easy, and it is I think reckless, to speak of "the logic of liberalism" (even if it is responsible to speak of Benthamite or Hayekian logic, or the logic of Mill's *On Liberty*). At a minimum, we need a specification of what liberalism is. And if liberalism is characterized in certain ways, it might turn out to be unappealing, even to liberals.

We should not be surprised to see that some critics of liberalism offer accounts that liberalism's defenders would not embrace or even recognize. Such defenders might respond: "If liberalism meant what you say, I wouldn't much like it, either." Critics of liberalism might answer that their account is actually true to liberalism in both theory and practice, or that the account embraced by defenders of liberalism is not meaningfully different from the account(s) they reject. It might turn out to be difficult for such critics to defend those answers.

My main focus here is not on normative claims but on causal claims: about what liberalism has done, brought about, or ruined. People who are not friendly to liberalism on normative grounds have also made arguments about the social effects of "liberalism," which are said to include a growth in out-of-wedlock childbirth, lower marriage rates, higher divorce rates, repudiation of traditions, a rise in populism, economic inequality, deterioration of civic associations, political correctness, hostility or indifference to religion, and a general sense of social alienation and rootlessness.[4] These are often styled as empirical claims, with the implicit suggestion that "liberalism" is both a necessary and a sufficient condition for an assortment of negative outcomes.

This suggestion seems to be resonating in some circles. The problem is that liberalism is neither a person nor an agent but a constellation of ideas. A causal explanation of negative outcomes or trends must depend on the identification and investigation of competing hypotheses and an encounter with the evidence. We cannot, in the abstract, rule out the possibility that liberalism is actually responsible for one or another trend, just as we cannot rule out the possibility that the real culprit is misogyny, racism, feminism, capitalism, atheism, rock music, political correctness, television, economic growth, modern birth control, the iPhone, Facebook, or the Internet. Even so, the idea that liberalism is responsible for lower marriage rates, the rise of Donald Trump, Brexit, populism in Europe, same-sex marriage, high rates of economic growth, low rates of economic growth, or speech codes on university campuses is puzzling and even reckless. To defend such ideas, we would need a specification of what liberalism is and (what would be exceptionally difficult) an account of how it brought about or led to the relevant outcomes. It is hardly enough to observe, for example, that defenders of same-sex marriage invoke something like Mill's harm principle or that Bentham was enthusiastic about immigration.

I am aware that I have been offering some brisk notes on a complex topic. I will not go far beyond them here, but I will offer an elaboration with reference to some lively and provocative remarks made by Yoram Hazony in his 2019 Vaughan Lecture delivered at Harvard Law School.[5] Hazony's ideas are worth engaging not only for their own sake but also because they overlap with, and offer a window on, broad strands of thinking about liberalism and its consequences.

Hazony's central goal is to provide a vivid narrative about the United States from the 1940s to the present. The tale involves some kind of fall, in which something he characterizes as bad and potentially dangerous (Enlightenment rationalism and liberalism) has triumphed over something he characterizes as good (tradition). In the process, rationalism and liberalism have been crushing both conservatism and religion. The result is a revolution that, if not deflected, "will end with the destruction of the Western democracies." The apocalyptic tone is not atypical of those who speak of liberalism as a baleful historical force (though for some writers, a large-scale collapse, even a kind of apocalypse, seems to be welcome).[6]

To make progress on the empirical arguments here, let us consider three subordinate claims. Hazony puts them in particularly clear and concise form, with an emphasis on the importance of tradition. But versions of those claims can be found in many places.

First, Hazony says that "liberalism has proved itself either unwilling or unable to successfully defend almost *any* inherited political ideals or norms, no matter how beneficial or useful they may be, once a focused attack on them has been under way for twenty or thirty years." He adds that we have witnessed "the serial destruction of all inherited concepts."

That, I think, is a challenging claim to defend. Literally countless inherited concepts are alive and well. Consider some inherited ideals, norms, and concepts that (many) liberals have defended, often successfully, in the face of focused attack: republican self-government, checks and balances, freedom of speech, freedom of religion, freedom from unreasonable searches and seizures, due process of law, equal protection, private property.

Once more: liberalism is a constellation of ideas. Its proponents are fully able to defend inherited political ideals and norms, and they often do. To be sure, they do not think it *adequate* to say that an ideal has been in place for a long time. But they agree that if an ideal has longevity on its side, there might be a lot to say in its favor. Both Hayek and Edmund Burke offered powerful arguments on that count, and nothing in liberalism is inconsistent with their arguments.[7] In fact, many liberals embrace them.

Second, Hazony argues that societies need not only freedom but constraints. He is certainly right on that count. But is it right to suggest that the "famous capacity for self-constraint has been disappearing"? To come to terms with that question, we need to ask: self-constraint with respect to what? In important places, there appear to be increases in self-constraint, and liberals of various kinds have supported them. Consider, for example, sexual violence, lynching, physical abuse of children, sexual harassment, smoking, drinking, littering, anti-Semitism, and spitting. All of these are more constrained than they were in the 1940s. We can see self-constraint as disappearing only if we focus on specific areas of life in which that has happened. If we did, we would see less self-constraint with respect to, say, body ornamentation or revealing one's sexual orientation—but more with respect to expressing ethnic prejudices. It would take a great deal of work, and some kind of metric or index, to establish that there is less self-constraint now than there was in 1945.

Because this point seems difficult to dispute, perhaps the real claim is about the weakening in the constraints of tradition, taken as such. If so, there is reason to be doubtful, for reasons taken up below. We might conclude that the problem lies not in the weakening of constraints in general but in the weakening of specific kinds of constraints—perhaps, for example, sex and marriage. To know whether constraints are disappearing in those areas, we would need data, and the evidence strongly suggests that in the domain of sex, constraints are growing, not loosening; compared to the 1960s and 1970s we seem to be in a "sex recession."[8] Is liberalism responsible for that?

But again, it is challenging to connect the loosening of constraints in any area to liberalism as such. We might be tempted to think that liberals are committed to freedom of choice and that that commitment has helped facilitate practices that liberalism's recent critics find troubling or worse. (Candidates include divorce, abortion, promiscuity, and same-sex marriage.) The question remains: can we really point to a causal chain between liberalism (in some form) and those practices?

Hazony claims that conservative thought suggests that people need constraint as well as freedom. That is true and important. Liberalism suggests the same thing. Liberals famously call for prohibitions on harm to others.[9] But liberals have also emphasized the importance of social norms, among other things to protect people from their own impulsiveness. Many of the examples invoked by critics of liberalism are easily fit within liberal accounts of constraint via law and norms.[10] Some liberals vigorously defend constraints on freedom, pointing to both autonomy and welfare.

Third, Hazony is entirely right, and onto something deeply important, in emphasizing the importance of honor. But it is not easy to defend the proposition that "honor has largely disappeared because it violates the Enlightenment sense that all must be regarded as equals." The term the *Greatest Generation*, coined in 1998 (by a liberal), is used to describe and honor those who fought and won World War II.[11] The term has become a matter of everyday language, and hurray for that. You can believe that all human beings have equal dignity while also honoring James Madison, Abraham Lincoln, Martin Luther King Jr., Rosa Parks, John McCain, and all those who fought for our nation at war.

There is no inconsistency there. Liberals do not think it is impossible "to justify publicly praising certain choices and not others."[12]

Let me speak a bit more broadly. Enlightenment rationalism is not a person. Liberalism is not an agent in history. It is not easy to defend the proposition that either is responsible for the legalization of abortion, same-sex marriage, or the elimination of prayer from the public schools.

Burke did not defy the Enlightenment or repudiate liberalism when he wrote, "We are afraid to put men to live and trade each on his own private stock of reason; because we suspect that this stock in each man is small, and that the individuals would do better to avail themselves of the general bank and capital of nations and of ages."[13] Many liberals are keenly aware that there are good reasons for Burkeanism. If a practice has stood the test of time, it might well be contributing to important social goals. If many people have endorsed a practice, we have epistemic reason to think that it makes sense.[14] But with respect to a long-standing norm or practice, it is always fair to ask: why?[15]

I return to my more general point. Some people see history as a war of "isms"—liberalism, conservativism, traditionalism, Marxism. We might say that they are committed to Ismism, contending that concrete historical developments are a product of some ism, or a conflict of isms, whether or not those contentions can be grounded in causal demonstrations. The narratives to which they are drawn tend to be grand and sweeping, and to many people seductive, even thrilling. They see the movements of societies as resulting from the triumph of abstract ideas, without showing how those ideas actually produced those movements.

The resulting accounts are often Manichean. The relevant isms tend to be invented rather than found. Those who speak in these ways tend to see one ism as very bad and another as very good. If their accounts are meant as explanations of how history has unfolded, they tend to be highly speculative: vivid, arresting tales that overlook what usually moves nations over years and decades, which are specific events, specific discoveries, specific interactions, specific technology, and specific people. Few of these—perhaps none of them—march to the tune of some ism. No one should deny that ideas matter, and as an assortment of ideas, liberalism matters a great deal. But to what, exactly?

Some historical accounts of the bad done by some ism, and the good promised by another, are really not historical explanations at all. Instead they are *normative* accounts. They are not about what caused what. Instead they are statements of conviction—opposition to one ism and support for another. Normative claims should be defended on normative grounds, not by reference to implausible claims about causation.

NINE

"Who Will Stop Me?"

The Cult of Ayn Rand

As a teenager, I fell for Ayn Rand.

More precisely, I fell for her novels. Reading *The Fountainhead* at the age of fourteen, I was overwhelmed by the passionate intensity of Rand's heroic characters.[1] Who could forget the indomitable Howard Roark? "His face was like a law of nature—a thing one could not question, alter or implore. It had high cheekbones over gaunt, hollow cheeks; gray eyes, cold and steady; a contemptuous mouth, shut tight, the mouth of an executioner or a saint." Roark was defined by his fierce independence: "I do not recognize anyone's right to one minute of my life. Nor to any part of my energy. Nor to any achievement of mine. No matter who makes the claim, how large their number or how great their need." Like countless teenage boys, I aspired to be like Roark. And I found Rand's heroine, Dominique Francon, irresistible. She was not only impossibly beautiful but brilliant, elegant, imperious, and cruel. "She looked like a stylized drawing of a woman and made the correct proportions of a normal being appear heavy and awkward beside her."

In Rand's operatic tales, the world is divided into two kinds of people: creators and parasites. The creator is "self-sufficient, self-motivated, self-generated." His only need is independence. He lives for himself. By contrast, the parasite "lives second-hand" and depends on other people. The parasite "preaches altruism"— a degrading thing—and "demands that man live for others."

At first I was thrilled by Rand's narratives, in which insidious parasites tried desperately to domesticate or enfeeble the creators, who ultimately found a way to triumph by carving out their own paths. Rand seemed to reveal secrets. She turned the world upside down. But after a few weeks of being enraptured with her work, her books started to sicken me. Contemptuous toward most of humanity, merciless about human frailty, and constantly hammering on the moral evils of redistribution, they produced a sense of claustrophobia. They had little humor or play. It wasn't that I detected a flaw in Rand's logic and decided to embrace altruism, or that I began to like the New Deal and the welfare state. It was more visceral than that. Reading and thinking about her novels was like being trapped in an elevator with someone who talked too loud, kept saying the same thing, and wouldn't shut up.

Decades later, I am struck by a puzzle. While Rand did not offer even a single interesting argument, her novels continue to resonate. She is a norm entrepreneur, and her novels change norms. They alter people's sense of what is normal and, in the process, change lives. They speak directly to an important part of the human soul. How does that happen?

President Donald Trump, a big Rand fan, has said that he identifies with Roark. *The Fountainhead,* he claims, "relates to business [and] beauty [and] life and inner emotions. That book relates to . . . everything." If we want to understand Trump, the widespread current contempt for "losers," and how the U.S. Congress can enact tax reform that greatly increases economic inequality, we might focus on Rand, whose "dour visage," as the cultural critic Lisa Duggan writes, "presides over the spirit of our time."[2] As Duggan puts it, Rand "made acquisitive capitalism sexy. She launched thousands of teenage libidos into the world of reactionary politics on a wave of quivering excitement."

Since it was published in 1943, *The Fountainhead* has sold over 6.5 million copies worldwide. *Atlas Shrugged,* generally regarded as Rand's most influential book, has done even better, with sales in excess of 7 million.[3] Prominent politicians express their admiration for her work. Secretary of State Mike Pompeo has said that *Atlas Shrugged* "really had an impact on me." Paul Ryan, the former Speaker of the House, once professed, "The reason I got involved in public service, by and large, if I had to credit one thinker, one person, it would be Ayn Rand."[4] Steve Jobs, Peter Thiel, and Jeff Bezos have all called themselves fans. As her biographer Jennifer Burns puts it, "For over half a century Rand has been the ultimate gateway drug to life on the right." Many people take her books, Burns adds, as "a sort of scripture."[5] American politics and the contemporary Republican Party owe a lot to Ayn Rand.

She was born Alissa Zinovievna Rosenbaum in 1905 in Saint Petersburg to a prosperous Jewish family. At thirteen she declared herself an atheist. (As she later put it, she rejected the idea that God was "the greatest entity in the universe. That made man inferior and I resented the idea that man was inferior to anything.") When the Bolshevik revolution came in 1917, it hit her family hard. The pharmacy her father owned was seized and nationalized. Rand's hatred of the Bolsheviks helped define her thinking about capitalism and redistribution. "I was twelve years old when I heard the slogan that man must live for the state," she later wrote, "and I thought right then and there that this idea was evil and the root of all the other evils we were seeing around us. I was already an individualist."[6]

The Bolshevik government shaped her future course, too, by exposing her to film. The Bolsheviks gave a great deal of support to the film industry, and Rand was enthralled by the potential of cinema and by what she was able to see of Hollywood movies. In 1924, she enrolled in a state institute to learn screenwriting and decided to go to the United States in the hope of becoming a screenwriter and novelist. She applied for a passport and got it. She also obtained a U.S. visa, falsely telling a U.S. consular official that she was engaged to a Russian man and would undoubtedly return. In 1926, she left Soviet Russia. She never saw her parents again.

Not long after arriving in New York, she changed her name

to Ayn Rand. (How did she come up with that particular name? There has been much speculation but no authoritative answer.) She soon moved to Hollywood and quickly managed to meet her favorite director, Cecil B. DeMille (it is not clear how); he hired her as a junior screenwriter. She also met Frank O'Connor, a devastatingly handsome, elegant, unintellectual, mostly unsuccessful actor, of whom she said, "I took one look at him and, you know, Frank is the physical type of all my heroes. I instantly fell in love."[7] Reader, she stalked him. She and O'Connor married in 1929. They lived in California, and she continued to work as a screenwriter. From the very beginning, she was the family's breadwinner.

Rand's writing career picked up in the 1930s when she published her first two novels, *We the Living* and *Anthem*. (Rand enthusiasts regard both as classics.) Dismayed by the policies of President Franklin Delano Roosevelt and by what she saw as collectivist tendencies in American life, she avidly read FDR haters such as Albert Jay Nock and H. L. Mencken, who called themselves "libertarians" (understood as enthusiastic advocates of free markets and skeptics about state power, ultimately giving birth to an intellectual movement that has significantly influenced American politics). She began to write in defense of capitalism. In 1941, she produced a statement of principles, the Individualist Manifesto, meant as an alternative to the Communist Manifesto. These principles echoed throughout her work for the rest of her life. A sample:

The right of liberty means man's right to individual action, individual choice, individual initiative and individual property. Without the right to private property no independent action is possible.

The right to the pursuit of happiness means man's right to live for himself, to choose what constitutes his own, private, personal happiness and to work for its achievement. Each individual is the sole and final judge in this choice. A man's happiness cannot be prescribed to him by another man or by any number of other men.[8]

Written under the shadow of the manifesto and mostly in a one-year spurt of creativity, *The Fountainhead* was published in 1943. It became a sensation, largely through word of mouth. Readers described their reactions with words like *awakening* and *revelation*. Rand became a celebrity almost overnight. People wanted to meet her—men in particular. It is unclear whether her relationship with any of those men turned sexual, but there were serious flirtations and apparently romantic feelings. Her husband's acting career was going poorly, and he was economically dependent on his wife; in many ways, their marriage represented a reversal of traditional sex roles. Rand wasn't living the man-worship depicted in her novels.

After World War II, Rand became an anti-Communist Cold Warrior, testifying before the House Un-American Activities Committee about Communist infiltration of the film industry. In 1944 she started to write *Atlas Shrugged;* it took her thirteen years to finish. In that period, Rand withdrew from the political fray and relied on a small social circle created for her by her most trusted acolyte, Nathan Blumenthal. Blumenthal, who worked part-time as a psychologist using Rand's principles, was a handsome and vibrant Canadian who had long idolized her. Twenty-five years younger than Rand, he had read and reread *The Fountainhead* at the age of fourteen, memorizing whole passages. (Been there, done that.) In high school and then as a student at the University of California at Los Angeles, he wrote fan letters to Rand. After first ignoring them, in 1950 she invited the nineteen-year-old undergraduate to visit.

Sparks flew when Blumenthal and Rand first met, at least by his account. "I felt as if ordinary reality had been left somewhere behind," he later wrote, "and I was entering the dimension of my most passionate longing."[9] They talked philosophy from 8 that night until 5:30 the next morning, while Frank sat by in silence. Blumenthal described himself as "intoxicated"—"two souls . . . shocked by mutual recognition." A few hours after the meeting, still early in the morning, he went to the apartment of his girlfriend Barbara Weidman, also a Rand enthusiast. He was rapturous. "She's fascinating," he told Weidman. "She's Mrs. Logic." A week later, Blumenthal returned to Rand's home, this time with Weidman, who reported that she "was not a conventionally attractive woman, but compelling in the remarkable combination of perceptiveness and sensuality, of intelligence and passionate intensity, that she projected."

Soon Blumenthal and Rand were speaking almost every evening, sometimes for hours. The two couples—Ayn and Frank,

Nathan and Barbara—became close, even intimate. In 1951, Nathan and Barbara moved to New York to study at New York University. Ayn and Frank joined them a few months later.

These were the founding members of Rand's philosophical movement, which she called objectivism. Things definitely got weird, beginning to take on aspects of a personality cult. Nathan Blumenthal, with Rand's endorsement, decided to change his name to Nathaniel Branden, exclaiming, "Why should we be stuck with someone else's choice of name?"[10] In January 1953, he married Barbara Weiden, with Rand as matron of honor and Frank as best man. Barbara took the invented last name, too.

In September 1954, Ayn and Nathaniel declared to their spouses that they had fallen in love with each other, and Rand, the apostle of reason, calmly informed Barbara and Frank that it was only rational that they should fall in love themselves. As Rand put it, "If Nathan and I are who we are, if we see what we see in each other, if we truly hold the values we profess, how can we not be in love?" But she promised that despite their feelings, the relationship between the two of them would not be physical. "We have no future, except as friends," she told Barbara and Frank. Predictably, their relationship did turn sexual.[11] But Ayn and Frank stayed married, as did Barbara and Nathaniel. Throughout the period, Rand worked intensely on *Atlas Shrugged*; Frank and both Brandens read multiple drafts.

Over a thousand pages long, the book is dystopian science fiction in which an imaginary U.S. government has asserted almost complete regulatory control over the private sector. Its first line

signals a mystery: "Who is John Galt?" Society's godlike creators (inventors, scientists, thinkers, architects, and others who
do and make things), led by Galt, a Roark-like hero, decide to go
on strike. They withdraw from society and watch the parasites
and looters devour themselves. Ultimately the government collapses, and Galt plans to create a new society based on principles
of individualism. The final sentence of *Atlas Shrugged* captures
Galt in a moment of mastery: "He raised his hand, and over the
desolate earth he traced in space the sign of the dollar."

Rand dedicated her book to two people: her husband and
Nathaniel Branden. Of Branden, she wrote: "When I wrote *The
Fountainhead*, I was addressing myself to an ideal reader—to as
rational and independent a mind as I could conceive of. I found
such a reader—through a fan letter he wrote me about *The Fountainhead* when he was nineteen years old. He is my intellectual
heir. His name is Nathaniel Branden."[12]

Rand predicted that *Atlas Shrugged* would "be the most controversial book of this century; I'm going to be hated, vilified,
lied about, smeared in every possible way." The early reviews
fulfilled these expectations. The most severe came from *National
Review*, where Whittaker Chambers, the ex-Communist and conservative hero, deplored her atheism and proclaimed: "Out of
a lifetime of reading, I can recall no other book in which a tone
of overriding arrogance is so implacably sustained. . . . From almost any page of *Atlas Shrugged*, a voice can be heard from pain-
ful necessity, commanding: 'To a gas chamber—go!'"[13]

The book became a national phenomenon, but Rand was devastated. She craved approval not from ordinary readers but from prominent thinkers, including academics, and she didn't get it. She fell into a deep depression, telling the Brandens, "John Galt wouldn't feel like this."[14] (She didn't mean this as a joke. Rand didn't do self-deprecation.) She never wrote fiction again. Nathaniel Branden became a vigorous entrepreneur on her behalf, organizing objectivism into various lecture series, and in 1961 creating the Nathaniel Branden Institute (NBI) in homage to her. Four years later, the Brandens separated as a couple, but they continued to work closely together as, in Barbara's words, "comrades in arms." They succeeded in producing something like an organized movement, with thirty-five hundred student followers in fifty cities by 1967. The NBI, and Rand's social world, revolved around what she called the Collective, a small group of devotees that included Alan Greenspan, who went on to become chairman of the Federal Reserve Board.

But something was rotten in the state of NBI. There was secrecy—the organization was led by Rand and Branden, whose passionate, turbulent relationship was known to their spouses but hidden from everyone else—and there was enforced orthodoxy. Within the Collective and the NBI, Rand and Branden would not tolerate the slightest dissent. As Branden wrote in his memoir with a kind of mordant humor, students were taught the following:

- Ayn Rand is the greatest human being who has ever lived.

- *Atlas Shrugged* is the greatest human achievement in the history of the world.
- Ayn Rand, by virtue of her philosophical genius, is the supreme arbiter in any issue pertaining to what is rational, moral, or appropriate to man's life on earth.

In 1968, things fell to pieces. Rand abruptly split with the Brandens, stating in a bizarre, unhinged public letter, "I hereby withdraw my endorsement of them and of their future works and activities. I repudiate both of them, totally and permanently, as spokesmen for me or for Objectivism."[15] Though she referred to various financial and personal improprieties, she did not disclose the actual reasons for the split. Both Brandens responded with public letters of their own. Neither revealed the truth, which was intensely personal. While working closely with Rand and continuing to proclaim his love for her, Nathaniel had ended their sexual relationship, citing supposed psychological problems (for which she "counseled" him). All the while, he was having a secret love affair with another woman. He disclosed that relationship to Barbara as early as 1966; after repeated entreaties from Rand, in which she asked what on earth was wrong with Nathaniel, Barbara told her the truth.

Rand was shattered. Branden, she told Barbara, had taken away "this earth." She fell into an implacable rage, which lasted for the rest of her life. She never spoke to Nathaniel Branden again. Barbara put it this way to Nathaniel: "Ayn wants you dead." Among other things, she ordered the deletion of her glowing dedication to Nathaniel in subsequent printings of *Atlas Shrugged.*

Despite her emotional devastation, Rand continued to work and to write. She spoke on college campuses and did interviews on television, where she was often engaging, charming, and even funny. She wrote long essays for the *Objectivist* magazine and the *Ayn Rand Letter.*

In the 1970s her health deteriorated. A lifelong smoker, she was diagnosed with lung cancer in 1974. Five years later, Frank O'Connor died, again shattering her. Rand herself died in 1982. By that point, she had alienated or rejected most of her friends.

Since the crash of 2008, Rand's works have experienced a revival of popularity; her books have been selling astonishingly well. *Atlas Shrugged* sold five hundred thousand copies in 2009, more than doubling the previous record for highest sales, established the year prior. In some respects the age of Trump can be seen as the age of Rand. Trump is anything but a self-made man, but some of his policies are unmistakably Randian: tax cuts, especially for the wealthy; elimination of safeguards for consumers and workers; repeal of environmental regulations.

Rand influenced contemporary political thought and affected people's conception of the normal less through her ideas than because she offered, in *The Fountainhead* and *Atlas Shrugged,* heroic accounts of capitalism and capitalists, whom she contrasted with the losers, moochers, and "second-handers" who seek to steal from them through taxes and regulation. She gave voice to, and helped spur, a specifically moral objection to redistribution of wealth and to interference with property rights and market arrangements. That objection resonates strongly in the business community and the Republican Party, and something like it has fervent advocates in the Trump administration.

Was Rand a serious thinker? That is doubtful. She did not defend her conclusions so much as pound the table for them. Yet she did write a great deal in an effort to justify objectivism in strictly philosophical terms. Robert Nozick, the influential libertarian philosopher, seemed to take her seriously, and the Ayn Rand Society, affiliated with the American Philosophical Association, produces papers and books focusing on her work. But anyone interested in free markets, liberty of contract, and the importance of private property would do a lot better to read Friedrich Hayek, Milton Friedman, or Nozick himself.

Rand's enduring influence comes from her fiction—from her ability to capture the sheer exhilaration of personal defiance, human independence, and freedom from chains of all kinds. Rand touched and legitimated the psychological roots of a prominent strand in right-wing thought. A skeptic about Roark's ambitious plans poses this question to him: "My dear fellow, who will let you?" Roark's answer: "That's not the point. The point is, who will stop me?" That exchange captures what many people think is not merely wrong but evil about Roosevelt's New Deal, the Affordable Care Act, the Consumer Financial Protection Bureau, the Clean Air Act, even the Civil Rights Act of 1964. Call it Who Will Stop Me? Capitalism. It has special resonance among adolescent boys, but its appeal is much broader than that. The problem is that those who need to lionize men with "a contemptuous mouth, shut tight, the mouth of an executioner or a saint" tend to be terrified of something. Altruism really is okay. Redistribution to those who need help is not a violation of human rights.

Rand had a unique talent for transforming people's political convictions through tales of indomitable heroes and heroines, romance, and sex. Her novels have been described as "conversion machines that run on lust."[16] Decades after Rand's death, Branden seemed to agree. "[Not] just Ayn and me," he wrote, "but all of us—we were ecstasy addicts. No one ever named it that way, but that was the key."

TEN

History's Forks

How differently would things have turned out if George Washington had made some terrible strategic decisions during the Revolutionary War, if Adolf Hitler had been assassinated, if Harry Truman had not used the atom bomb, if Ronald Reagan had had more success as an actor, if the attacks of 9/11 had failed, or if Donald Trump had decided to stay in real estate? Part of the fascination of counterfactual history lies in the possibility that relatively small differences, not merely large ones, could have altered the arc of whole nations. If someone had said a firm "no" to Hitler or Reagan at a certain stage, or if someone had said "yes" to people we have never heard of, might the world look radically different?

Consider an example from 2020. Former vice president Joe Biden was running for president. His campaign was going very poorly. He had lost the early primaries in Iowa, New Hampshire, and Nevada. Senator Bernie Sanders was looking highly likely to win. A lot of smart people thought that the nomination battle was over. Representative Jim Clyburn of South Carolina endorsed Biden shortly before the South Carolina primary, and that spurred a flood of votes for Biden—many from African Americans, but many from others who trusted Clyburn. The result was a massive win for Biden in South Carolina, which created a kind of cascade in Biden's favor. We cannot know for sure, but it's reasonable to think that without Clyburn's endorsement, Sanders would have won the nomination. If so, who knows how American history would have unfolded?

These questions are not only fun but also fascinating, not least because they connect large historical inquiries with ordinary life, where unexpected forks in the road, and sheer serendipity, seem to move us in unanticipated directions. (How did you end up in your job? In your city? With your current or most recent romantic partner?) And there are deeper points. Questions about counterfactual history raise philosophical puzzles about the nature of causation: what does it mean to say that one thing, or one event, "caused" another?[1] There are related issues, discussed by David Lewis and Jon Elster, about the nature of possible worlds.[2]

Behavioral scientists emphasize "hindsight bias," which means that after an event has happened, people tend to think that it was inevitable, or at least far more predictable than it actually was. "I knew it all along" is a reflection of hindsight bias, especially when people say it sincerely. Hindsight bias has often been studied in the context of smaller events, the stuff of personal life. But after a major political change happens, there is a human tendency to think that it was inevitable, and that the values and expectations the change brought to the fore were always going to emerge and dominate. Sometimes it takes a concerted effort of historical reconstruction to understand that this is far from true, and that the new values could easily have been rejected.

Many large-scale events—the election of one leader rather than a very different one, the success of a revolution, the outbreak of a war, the maintenance of peace, an international agreement— are a product of something like serendipity. A butterfly might have flapped its wings at just the right time. Someone might have cried, "Yes!" or "No!" in a highly visible way, helping to fuel a movement for a cause or a candidate, for liberation or its opposite. That person might make it into the history books; he or she might define an era. (Think Adolf Hitler, Fidel Castro, Martin Luther King Jr., Rosa Parks, Gloria Steinem.) But despite their importance, such people might remain unknown. Their own role might be largely invisible. One of the virtues of counterfactual history is that it weakens the power of hindsight bias. It shows us that what we take to be normal might be the result of something small or accidental, or at least something that might have been otherwise. That can be frightening. It can also be inspiring.

We can approach those issues by exploring the views of Richard Evans, an expert on the rise of Nazism and a skeptic about counterfactual history.[3] Evans treats counterfactualists as fundamentally unserious, barnacles on the profession of history, frivolous thinkers offering speculations that "tread on thin evidential ice." Most of his argument is sensible, wise, and convincing, and for those who are interested in history's forks, it contains important cautionary notes. But I want to offer a fundamental objection to his ultimate conclusion: for those who seek historical explanations, counterfactual history is inevitable. Any causal claim is an exercise of counterfactual history. Historians (professional or otherwise) are pervasively counterfactualists. That point bears on how we should think about democracy—its travails, its triumphs, its vulnerability, and its failures.

I approach this topic not only as a fan of science fiction but also as a teacher of law, where there is an extensive literature on the topic of causation and hence on possible worlds.[4] Suppose there was a car accident in which Jones was badly hurt. The accident occurred when Smith, who was drinking, ran a red light and hit Jones's vehicle, which was going well over the speed limit. Did Smith cause Jones's injury? As a legal matter, the likely answer is that he did. If Smith had not run the red light, Jones would not have been hurt—at least not when and as he was. If a judge finds that Smith was responsible for Jones's injury, that he caused it, he is necessarily engaging in counterfactual history. He is essentially saying that history had a kind of fork in it, such that if Smith had not run the red light, the world would have been radically different.

In law, counterfactual history is pervasive. Judges do it; juries do it; lawyers do it. Members of the Supreme Court do it. To have "standing" to sue the government, for example, a litigant must show that he or she suffered an injury from some official action. Suppose that a woman sues the local prosecutor's office for failing to take action to force her ex-husband to make child support payments. She argues that some law required the prosecutor to proceed against her ex-husband. The prosecutor's office might respond that even if it had acted, there is no guarantee that the ex-husband would have made those payments. Perhaps he would have refused or even gone to jail. Whether that response is convincing turns on counterfactual history. The court will have to ask whether the world would have been different, in the relevant respect, if the local prosecutor had acted against the ex-husband. It will have to rerun history counterfactually. Nor is there anything exotic about this problem. The question of standing frequently turns on issues of causation and hence requires investigation of counterfactuals.

Is history different from law in this respect? It might be, if the historian is simply describing what happened: Jimmy Carter was the American president, the economy sputtered, Iran took American hostages, Ronald Reagan became the Republican nominee, Reagan defeated Carter, and National Airport was renamed Ronald Reagan National Airport. But if the historian is a bit more ambitious and offers explanations along with narratives, causal claims will be unavoidable. The historian might contend that the two factors that cost Carter the 1980 election were the Iran hostage crisis and the primary challenge from Ted Kennedy. This unremarkable analysis involves an implicit counterfactual claim: if the hostage crisis had not happened or Ted Kennedy had not run against him for the Democratic nomination, Carter would have been reelected. Any causal claim inevitably involves counterfactual history. There is nothing dishonorable about that. Causal explanation is necessarily counterfactual history.

It is important to distinguish among several quite different objections. Some counterfactual narratives are wildly implausible because they are inconsistent with what we know to be true. Consider this speculation: if Al Gore, a strong environmentalist, had become president in 2001, the United States would have ratified an international agreement to regulate greenhouse gases and, with respect to climate change, the world would be fundamentally different from how it is today. The problem is that developing nations, including China and India, had long been unenthusiastic about such a treaty, and it is highly doubtful that the U.S. Senate would have ratified any agreement without their participation. Some counterfactual histories rest on an inadequate understanding of historical constraints. Evans rightly objects to work that ignores or downplays those constraints and thus offers counterfactual history that defies an understanding of historical context. With this point in mind, historians can rule certain forms of counterfactual history out of bounds, on the ground that they are pure fantasy.

Other forms suffer from a different problem: they depend on such wildly elaborate causal chains that they are best treated as the exercise of an active imagination. Some counterfactualists suggest that if some apparently trivial change had occurred, large consequences would have followed ("the butterfly effect," made famous by a short story by Ray Bradbury). Logically, it may not be possible to rule out such elaborate causal chains, but they require a large number of contingencies to come to fruition (and, equally important, a large number of other contingencies not to do so). Consider, for example, Barbara Tuchman's suggestion that if Mao Zedong and Zhou Enlai had met with Franklin Delano Roosevelt in the 1940s, the wars in Korea and Vietnam might not have happened, or Geoffrey Parker's claim that if the Spanish Armada had successfully landed in England in 1588, Philip II would have established Spanish rule in North America. Maybe Tuchman and Parker are right—but who could possibly know?[5]

Still other counterfactuals depend on a change that cannot logically be made without simultaneously introducing, or allowing the possibility of, other relevant changes that the counterfactualist is attempting to bracket. Once we introduce some changes, all bets are off. It is not helpful to ask what would have happened if the iPad had been invented right before the Great Depression. Gloria Steinem offered a memorable counterfactual: "If men could get pregnant, abortion would be a sacrament." But if men could get pregnant, they would not be men, at least not in the familiar sense, and in a world in which men's reproductive capacities were the same as women's, we really cannot say much about the legal status of abortion.

The most fantastic counterfactual narratives fall in this category. If Nazi Germany had cell phones, Hitler might have won the war—but if Nazi Germany had cell phones, the world would be so unrecognizably different that it is not clear that we can say anything at all. If horses were smarter than people, they might rule the world. As Niall Ferguson writes, "No sensible person wishes to know what would have happened in 1948 if the entire population of Paris had suddenly sprouted wings."[6] (Though, come to think of it, that's a pretty interesting question.)

We can therefore dismiss counterfactual history when it is based on false historical claims, wildly elaborate causal chains, or all-bets-are-off changes. But what if it is vulnerable to none of these objections? Evans does not give a satisfactory answer to this question. Not long ago, President Obama and his advisers made a series of decisions without which the United States, and the world, would be different. In 2010, for example, Obama decided to push for enactment of the Affordable Care Act, rejecting the reported advice of Vice President Biden and Chief of Staff Rahm Emanuel that he focus only on combating the Great Recession. It is legitimate and even instructive to ask how things might have turned out if Obama had been persuaded.

In their superb anthology on the topic, Philip Tetlock and Aaron Belkin specify a set of criteria for assessing counterfactual arguments. Tetlock and Belkin rightly urge, "We can avoid counterfactuals only if we eschew all causal inference and limit ourselves to strictly noncausal narratives of what actually happened."[7] To discipline counterfactual history, they emphasize the importance of well-specified antecedents and consequents, of logical consistency among connecting principles, of avoiding preposterous claims about causality, and of maintaining consistency with well-established historical facts.[8] Econometricians like Robert Fogel have used statistical tools to produce counterfactual histories, and while Evans wants to bracket their work, it is not clear how he can do so.[9] Many econometricians have produced the equivalent of counterfactual history, aided by careful statistical analysis.[10]

The most fundamental problem is that many historians offer not only narratives but also explanations. They say that some event—the rise of Nazism, the Vietnam War, the election of Ronald Reagan, the attacks of 9/11—had particular causes. It is not possible to take a stand on the existence of causes, or on their relative importance, without thinking about what the world would be like if one or another were removed. If we say that the Vietnam War or the passage of the Civil Rights Act of 1964 was "caused" by the Kennedy assassination, we must imagine a world in which Kennedy was not assassinated. We inevitably introduce counterfactual history: we are making a claim about what would have happened in that alternative and historically unrealized world. This is so whenever historians speak of causes and explanations.

Evans himself is no exception. In responding to Ferguson's argument about the consequences of British neutrality in 1914, he offers some counterfactual history of his own. (To be sure, his account is tentative, but counterfactual history generally ought to be tentative.) He suggests that if Britain had stayed out of the war, Germany would not have scaled back its war aims. And in response to John Charmley's arguments about the potentially beneficial effects of appeasing Hitler, he suggests that Germany would have attacked Britain in any case, with a higher probability of victory. He appears to support Churchill's suggestion that Britain could have become a "slave state." True, his statements on these counts are qualified and cautious, but in explaining the rise of Nazism (an area in which he has extraordinary expertise), Evans writes more firmly, saying that the "key factor" was "the Nazi's storm troopers' escalating use of violence"—which seems to be an unambiguous suggestion that absent that violence, the Nazis might not have come to power.[11] He also speculates that with "more skillful maneuvering by men like General Schleicher," a representative of the army, rather than Hitler, might have ended up running Germany.

Or consider Evans's attempt to explain the explosion of counterfactual history since the 1990s. In pointing to the decline of grand ideologies and the rise of postmodernism, he is arguing that if the grand ideologies had not declined, and if postmodernism had not arisen, we would have seen less counterfactual history—which is itself counterfactual history.

Evans is hardly unaware of the claim that whenever historians designate a cause, they are implicitly using counterfactuals. In his view, however, "normally historians are not so bold as this," and they prefer to use the word *probably*. Is this sufficient? If historians say that a factor was "probably" a necessary condition, they are still engaging in counterfactual thinking, just qualifying it. Surely Evans would not withdraw his objections if Niall Ferguson, Charmley, and other counterfactualists had inserted "probably" in the appropriate places. Return to the context of law. If a court rules that Smith caused Jones's injury, it might be saying that Jones has proved, by a preponderance of the evidence, that Smith caused that injury. This is the same as saying that Smith "probably" caused the injury. Claims about causation are always probabilistic, even if the probability is sometimes very high.

Evans adds that even when historians call a "cause necessary rather than possible or contributory, they almost never speculate about the alternative course events might have taken had it not been operative." This misses the point. Whenever historians call a cause necessary, they are, by virtue of that very statement, speculating about an alternative course.

Here is another way to make the point. Social scientists test hypotheses. They might hypothesize, for example, that if people have to pay a small tax for plastic bags at convenience stores, they will use fewer plastic bags. They might say that if public officials ask people to sign forms at the beginning of the document rather than at the end, they are less likely to lie on the forms. To test hypotheses, social scientists usually prefer to conduct randomized controlled trials, allowing them to isolate the effects of the tax or signatures at the beginning of forms. Such trials actually create little parallel worlds and hence alternative histories—one with the tax and one without it, one with signatures at the beginning and one with signatures at the end. To that extent, social scientists create the equivalent of counterfactual worlds.

Historians cannot conduct randomized controlled trials, because history is run only once. Yet they often develop hypotheses and attempt to evaluate them by reference to the evidence. Evans is himself engaged in this enterprise. Causal hypotheses venture counterfactual inferences. Any claim of causation requires a statement that without the cause, the effect would not have occurred, at least not at the same time and in the same way. Recall that the legal system is replete with such statements, which account for many legal conclusions.

At this point, a skeptic might respond that once we specify a particular standard of proof—say, preponderance of the evidence—we might find that historians often lack the evidence to meet that standard. Some historical events are overdetermined. Factor A contributed to outcome Z (a war, an economic downturn), but so did factors B, C, D, and E, and if you remove A, and even B and C, Z nonetheless would have happened. Sometimes historians can identify contributing factors, but they cannot sort out which conditions are either necessary or sufficient.

Of course, that is sometimes true. But we can safely say that if President George W. Bush had been assassinated, Vice President Dick Cheney would have almost certainly become president, and we can safely say that if the Supreme Court had had an additional Republican nominee in 2011 (and one fewer Democratic appointee), the Affordable Care Act would probably have been struck down. To be sure, assessments of what would have followed those counterfactual events would be highly speculative. But I do not think that Evans wants to deny that historians have the ability to offer (some) causal explanations, and if he does, his target is a lot larger than the kind of counterfactual work that concerns him.

The problem is that in order to offer an explanation of what happened, historians have to identify causes, and whenever they identify causes, they immediately conjure up a counterfactual history, a parallel world. There is a lot of distance between science fiction novelists and the world's great historians, but along an important dimension they are playing the same game.

Epilogue

The power of the normal presents a paradox. On the one hand, people's judgments about an action or a situation are often a product of what else they see. If we are surrounded by brutality, a little cruelty might not much bother us. If we live in a very free society, a minor intrusion on our liberty might provoke outrage. What is normal provides the background against which we make judgments about the most fundamental moral, political, and legal questions.

On the other hand, what is normal can change in a hurry, and people get used to something new and radically different. People start to get sick from coronavirus, and the disease is contagious and potentially fatal, and the world shuts down. People wash their hands, a lot. They don't shake hands. They wear face masks. They stay at home. (#StayHome goes viral.) Information gets out about the harms of smoking, and in a short time, the norm changes: you don't smoke in the workplace (or in movie theaters, or trains, or airplanes). Someone draws attention to sexual harassment, and she starts a social cascade, making long-standing practices seem intolerable, a form of discrimination or worse.

The power of the normal stems, in large part, from our keen responsiveness to what others say and do. That responsiveness also helps explain why things can shift so quickly. Under the right conditions, what was unthinkable can become routine. Usually that takes a while, but not always, especially when the new normal seems necessary to avert disaster. If people perceive an external threat, or if their lives are on the line, a radical change in both thought and action will almost inevitably create a new normal.

Some of the social and political changes discussed here deserve widespread approval. Consider the ratification of the American Constitution, the movement for gender equality, even (I think) the rise of the administrative state, staffed in large part by experts and technocrats. Other changes, such as the rise of fascism, are dark stains on human history. However we evaluate them, many of those changes involve the same general mechanisms, including group polarization, informational cascades, and the unleashing of long-hidden preferences and values.

An appreciation of the paradox—the simultaneous power and fragility of the normal—attests to one fact above all: human beings are astonishingly resilient. We are capable of remarkable adaptation. What is normal on Monday might seem like ancient times by Friday. Even so, people find ways to cope. If that fact helps account for social horrors, and the success of authoritarian leaders, it also helps explain why people can live and flourish under the most difficult circumstances—and much of the time, find ways to make a better world.

Notes

ONE

Howling with the Wolves

1. Milton Mayer, *They Thought They Were Free: The Germans, 1933–1945* (Chicago: University of Chicago Press, 1955).
2. Sebastian Haffner, *Defying Hitler: A Memoir* (New York: Picador, 2003).
3. Timor Kuran, *Public Truths, Private Lies: The Social Consequences of Preference Falsification* (Cambridge, MA: Harvard University Press, 1997).
4. For the violation of the law in regard to lead paint, see *In re* A Community Voice, 878 F.3d 779 (9th Cir. 2017).

TWO

The New Normal

1. George Orwell, *Nineteen Eighty-Four* (London: Secker & Warburg, 1950).
2. David E. Levari et al., "Prevalence-Induced Concept Change," *Science*, no. 29 (2018): 1465–67.

THREE

Revolution Is in the Air

1. Timur Kuran, "The Inevitability of Future Revolutionary Surprises," *American Journal of Sociology* 100, no. 6 (1995): 1528–51.

2. Asef Bayat, "The Arab Spring and Its Surprises," *Development and Change*, no. 44 (2013): 587–601.

3. Kuran, "The Inevitability of Future Revolutionary Surprises"; Timur Kuran and Diego Romero, "The Logic of Revolutions: Rational Choice Perspective," in *The Oxford Handbook of Public Choice*, vol. 2, ed. Roger D. Congleton et al. (Oxford: Oxford University Press, 2019); Merouan Mekouar, *Protest and Mass Mobilization: Authoritarian Collapse and Political Change in North Africa* (New York: Routledge, 2016). For an emphasis on the importance of communications technologies, see Muzammil M. Hussain and Philip N. Howard, "What Best Explains Successful Protest Cascades?" *International Studies Review* 15, no. 1 (2013): 48–66.

4. There are many accounts. For especially good ones, see Kuran, "The Inevitability of Future Revolutionary Surprises"; D. Garth Taylor, "Pluralistic Ignorance and the Spiral of Silence: A Formal Analysis," *Public Opinion Quarterly* 46, no. 3 (1982): 311–35. A valuable account with special reference to law is Richard H. McAdams, *The Expressive Powers of Law: Theories and Limits* (Cambridge, MA: Harvard University Press, 2017), 136–62.

5. Wendy Pearlman, *We Crossed a Bridge and It Trembled: Voices from Syria* (New York: Custom House, 2017), 4.

6. Leonardo Bursztyn et al., "From Extreme to Mainstream: How Social Norms Unravel" (National Bureau of Economic Research Working Paper no. 23,415, Cambridge, MA, 2017), http://www.nber.org/papers/w23415.

7. The classic account is Mark Granovetter, "Threshold Models of Collective Behavior," *American Journal of Sociology* 83 (May 1978): 489–515; see also Kuran, "The Inevitability of Future Revolutionary Surprises."

8. Gordon S. Wood, *The Radicalism of the American Revolution* (New York: Vintage Books, 1991), 169.

9. Thomas Paine, "Letter to the Abbé Raynal," in *Life and Writings of Thomas Paine*, ed. Daniel Edwin Wheeler (New York: Vincent Parke, 1908), 242, quoted in Gordon Wood, *The Creation of the American Republic, 1776–1787* (Chapel Hill: University of North Carolina Press, 1998), 68.

10. Granovetter, "Threshold Models of Collective Behavior," remains the clearest explanation.

11. Seth Stephens-Davidowitz, *Everybody Lies* (New York: Dey Street Books, 2017).

12. Jon Elster, *Sour Grapes: Studies in Subversion of Rationality* (Cambridge: Cambridge University Press, 1983).

13. Choe Sang Hun, "North Korea #MeToo Voices: 'They Consider Us Toys,'" *New York Times*, October 31, 2018, https://www.nytimes.com/2018/10/31/world/asia/north-korea-women-metoo.html.

14. Kurt Weyland, "The Arab Spring: Why the Surprising Similarities with the Revolutionary Wave of 1848?" *Perspectives on Politics* 10, no. 4 (2012): 917–34.

15. Timur Kuran and Cass R. Sunstein, "Availability Cascades and Risk Regulation," *Stanford Law Review* 51, no. 4 (1999): 683–768.

FOUR

Lapidation and Apology

1. 8 John 1:11 (King James Version).
2. Darius Rejali, "Studying a Practice: An Inquiry into Lapidation," *Critique: Critical Middle Eastern Studies* 10, no. 18 (2001): 67–100.
3. Kate Taylor, "Harvard's First Black Faculty Deans Let Go amid Uproar over Harvey Weinstein Defense," *New York Times*, May 12, 2019, https://www.nytimes.com/2019/05/11/us/ronald-sullivan-harvard.html.
4. Richard Adams, "Cambridge College Sacks Researcher over Links with Far Right," *Guardian*, May 1, 2019, https://www.theguardian.com/education/2019/may/01/cambridge-university-college-dismisses-researcher-far-right-links-noah-carl.
5. Zack Beauchamp, "The Ilhan Omar Anti-Semitism Controversy, Explained," *Vox*, March 6, 2019, https://www.vox.com/policy-and-politics/2019/3/6/18251639/ilhan-omar-israel-anti-semitism-jews.
6. "Rep. Ilhan Omar Says She's Getting More Death Threats After Trump Tweet," *Los Angeles Times*, April 15, 2019, https://www.latimes.com/politics/la-na-pol-ilhan-omar-trump-tweet-9-11-story.html.
7. Gregory Krieg, "Here's the Deal with Elizabeth Warren's Native American Heritage," *CNN*, October 15, 2018, https://www.cnn.com/2016/06/29/politics/elizabeth-warren-native-american-pocahontas/index.html.
8. Elana Schor and Seung Min Kim, "Franken Resigns," *Politico*, December 7, 2017, https://www.politico.com/story/2017/12/07/franken-resigns-285957.
9. Vincent J. Rosivach, "Execution by Stoning in Athens," *Classical Antiquity* 6, no. 2 (1987): 232; Catherine E. Winiarski, "Adultery, Idolatry, and the Subject of Monotheism," *Religion & Literature* 38, no. 3 (2006): 44.
10. Jonathan Haidt, *The Righteous Mind: Why Good People Are Divided by Politics and Religion* (New York: Vintage Books, 2013).
11. Cass R. Sunstein, "The Law of Group Polarization," *Journal of Political Philosophy* 10 (2002): 176. I draw on that treatment here.
12. Roger Brown, *Social Psychology*, 2nd ed. (New York: Free Press, 1986), 224.
13. Craig McGarty et al., "Collective Action as the Material Expression of Opinion-Based Group Membership," *Journal of Social Issues* 65, no. 4 (2009): 851.
14. James Miller, *Democracy Is in the Streets: From Port Huron to the Siege of Chicago* (Cambridge, MA: Harvard University Press, 1987), 52.
15. Daniel Kahneman, *Thinking, Fast and Slow* (New York: Farrar, Straus & Giroux, 2011).

16. For references and discussion, see Cass R. Sunstein, *Why Nudge? The Politics of Libertarian Paternalism* (New Haven, CT: Yale University Press, 2015).
17. Tali Sharot, *The Optimism Bias: A Tour of the Irrationally Positive Brain* (New York: Vintage Books, 2011).
18. Herbert A. Simon, *Models of My Life* (New York: Basic Books, 1991), 281.
19. See Michael P. Haselhuhn et al., "How Implicit Beliefs Influence Trust Recovery," *Psychological Science* 21, no. 5 (2010): 645.
20. Richard Hanania, "Does Apologizing Work? An Empirical Test of the Conventional Wisdom," *Behavioral Public Policy*, October 23, 2019, https:// www.cambridge.org/core/journals/behavioural-public-policy/article/does -apologizing-work-an-empirical-test-of-the-conventional-wisdom/D34F1 D89E6FF6A6E32C22C75F0C5FE24.
21. For a start, see Cass R. Sunstein, "Falsehoods and the First Amendment," *Harvard Journal of Law and Technology* (forthcoming, 2020), https://papers .ssrn.com/sol3/papers.cfm?abstract_id=3426765&dgcid=ejournal_html email_u.s.:constitutional:law:rights:liberties:ejournal_abstractlink.
22. Hustler Magazine, Inc. v. Falwell, 485 U.S. 46 (1988).
23. Ibid.
24. New York Times Co. v. Sullivan, 376 U.S. 254 (1964); Gertz v. Robert Welch, Inc., 418 U.S. 323 (1974).
25. *Sullivan*, 376 U.S. at 279–80.
26. Chaplinsky v. New Hampshire, 315 U.S. 569 (1942); Gooding v. Wilson, 405 US 518 (1972). Note that the fighting words doctrine, as it is sometimes called, has not received serious attention from the Supreme Court for many decades. Modern forms of personal attack and bullying would appear to justify new attention.
27. Chaplinsky v. New Hampshire, 315 U.S. 569 (1942).
28. Hustler Magazine, Inc. v. Falwell, 485 U.S. 46 (1988).
29. Sunstein, "Falsehoods and the First Amendment." See also Facebook, "Community Standards," last visited March 16, 2020, https://www.facebook .com/communitystandards/bullying.
30. Ruth McGaffey, "The Heckler's Veto," *Marquette Law Review* 57, no. 1 (1973): 40.

FIVE

Founding

1. *The Federalist* (Cambridge, MA: Harvard University Press, 2009).
2. Montesquieu, *The Spirit of the Laws*, ed. Anne M. Cohler, Basia C. Miller, and Harold S. Stone (Cambridge: Cambridge University Press, 1989), chapter 2.1.

3. Gordon S. Wood, *The Radicalism of the American Revolution* (New York: Vintage Books, 1991).
4. Ibid., 29.
5. Ibid., 29–30.
6. Ibid., 6.
7. Ibid.
8. David Hume, "Whether the British Government Inclines More to Absolute Monarchy, or to a Republic," in *Complete Works of David Hume* (Hastings, UK: Delphi Classics, 2016).
9. Wood, *The Radicalism of the American Revolution*, 168.
10. Ibid, 169.
11. Ibid., 7.
12. Walt Whitman, *Leaves of Grass* (New York: Start, 2013).
13. Bob Dylan, "It's Alright Ma (I'm Only Bleeding)," in *Bringing It All Back Home* (New York: Columbia Records, 1965).
14. Montesquieu, *The Spirit of the Laws.*
15. Herbert Storing, ed., *The Complete Anti-Federalist* (Chicago: University of Chicago Press, 2007).
16. Ibid., 201.

SIX

Refounding

1. John Paul Stevens, *Six Amendments: How and Why We Should Change the Constitution* (New York: Little, Brown, 2014).
2. District of Columbia v. Heller, 554 U.S. 570 (2008).
3. Citizens United v. FEC, 558 U.S. 310 (2010).
4. Buckley v. Valeo, 424 U.S. 1 (1976).
5. Furman v. Georgia, 408 U.S. 238 (1972).
6. Gregg v. Georgia, 428 U.S. 153 (1976).
7. Rucho v. Common Cause, 139 S. Ct. 2484 (2019).
8. Printz v. United States, 521 U.S. 898 (1997).

SEVEN

Radicals

1. Jeremy McCarter, *Young Radicals: In the War for American Ideals* (New York: Random House, 2017).
2. Ibid., 72.
3. Quoted in Walter Lippmann, *Drift and Mastery: An Attempt to Diagnose the Current Unrest* (Madison: University of Wisconsin Press, 1961), 14.
4. Walter Lippmann, *Public Opinion* (New York: Free Press Paperbacks, 1997).

EIGHT
Liberalism

1. Anna Collar, *Religious Networks in the Roman Empire: The Spread of New Ideas* (Cambridge: Cambridge University Press, 2013). True, we can raise questions about whether Christianity is an "ism," and not only because of the contingent fact that the word does not end with those three letters.

2. Patrick J. Deneen, *Why Liberalism Failed* (New Haven, CT: Yale University Press, 2018). Yoram Hazony, *The Virtue of Nationalism* (New York: Basic Books, 2018), also has a spirited attack on liberalism, opposing it to nationalism. I am focusing on a particular kind of attack, but (intriguingly) overlapping efforts, usually coming from the political Left, are plentiful, and many of them are not recent. For evidence and clarification of the overlap, see Joseph Hogan, "The Problems of Liberalism: A Q&A with Patrick Deneen," *Nation*, May 28, 2018, https://www.thenation.com/article/the-problems-of-liberalism-a-qa-with-patrick-deneen/. Many of those efforts do not give a sufficiently clear or charitable account of what liberalism is, and they also claim that liberalism is responsible for concrete bad things; they count as forms of Ismism as I understand that idea here. See, for example, Uday Singh Mehta, *Liberalism and Empire* (Chicago: University of Chicago Press, 1999). Some interesting work might be done here on the history of ideas, with an emphasis on anti-liberal thought from radically different political foundations, but with related claims. An example of such work is Stephen Holmes, *The Anatomy of Antiliberalism* (Cambridge, MA: Harvard University Press, 1993), which makes many powerful points. Relevant in general is the discussion of "soft obscurantism" in Jon Elster, "Hard and Soft Obscurantism in the Humanities and Social Sciences," *Diogenes* 58, nos. 1–2 (2011): 159–70.

3. For an especially valuable account, see Martha C. Nussbaum, "Perfectionist Liberalism and Political Liberalism," *Philosophy & Public Affairs* 39, no. 1 (2011): 3–45; for a helpful overview, see Duncan Bell, "What Is Liberalism?" *Political Theory* 42, no. 6 (2014): 682–715. John Rawls, *Political Liberalism* (New York: Columbia University Press, 1993), remains defining; it is often ignored or mischaracterized in contemporary debates. As Nussbaum puts it, "The concept of political liberalism is simply ignored in a large proportion of discussions of welfare and social policy, as are the challenges Rawls poses to thinkers who would base politics on a single comprehensive normative view." Nussbaum, "Perfectionist Liberalism and Political Liberalism," 6. For an early statement, see Charles Larmore, *Patterns of Moral Complexity* (Cambridge: Cambridge University Press, 1987). Also valuable is Stephen Holmes, *Benjamin Constant and the Making of Modern Liberalism* (New Haven, CT: Yale University Press, 1984); Stephen Holmes, *Passions and Constraint* (Chicago: University of Chicago Press, 1995). A clear and

broad overview can be found in "Liberalism," in *Stanford Encyclopedia of Philosophy* (1996, revised 2018), https://plato.stanford.edu/entries/liberalism/.

4. Some of these claims can be found Deneen, *Why Liberalism Failed.*

5. Yoram Hazony, "A Confederacy of Prodigies: On the Ascending of Reason and the Extinction of Conservatism in America" (lecture presented at Harvard Law School, April 2, 2019).

6. This is so of Deneen, *Why Liberalism Failed*, and it is noteworthy that his prophecy of some kind of major upheaval or collapse seems, in some circles, to be welcome, exciting, in a sense even thrilling. See at xxvi–xxvii: "Liberalism created the conditions, and the tools, for its own worst nightmare. . . . Sacrifice and patience are not the hallmarks of the age of statist individualism. But they will be needed in abundance in order for us to usher in a better, doubtless very different, time after liberalism." See also at 191: "Already there is evidence of growing hunger for an organic alternative to the cold, bureaucratic, and mechanized world liberalism offers," and at 198: "After a five hundred–year philosophical experiment that has now run its course, the way is clear to building anew and better. The greatest proof of human freedom today lies in our ability to imagine, and build, liberty after liberalism." Deneen is no Marxist, but there is something in these words, and in various forms of Ismism, that have the same emotional tenor, the same kind of excitement, the same claims of historical inexorability (in the preferred directions), as Marxism.

7. See, for example, Friedrich Hayek, "The Origins and Effects of Our Morals: A Problem for Science," in *The Essence of Hayek*, ed. Chiaki Nishiyama and Kurt Leube (Stanford, CA: Hoover Institution Press, 1984), 318.

8. Kate Julian, "Why Are Young People Having so Little Sex?" *Atlantic*, December 2018, https://www.theatlantic.com/magazine/archive/2018/12/the-sex-recession/573949/.

9. The classic discussion is John Stuart Mill, "On Liberty," in *The Basic Writings of John Stuart Mill: On Liberty, the Subjection of Women, and Utilitarianism*, ed. Dale E. Miller (New York: Random House, 2002). For those who believe in the claims of tradition, Mill is a fair (normative) target. The challenge is to defend the proposition that Mill or Millianism—which should not be identified with liberalism—is causally responsible for actual outcomes that they abhor.

10. Edna Ullmann-Margalit, *The Emergence of Norms* (Oxford: Oxford University Press, 1977).

11. Tom Brokaw, *The Greatest Generation* (New York: Random House, 2001).

12. Admittedly, some complexities are raised by the account in John Rawls, *A Theory of Justice* (Cambridge, MA: Belknap, 1971), at least insofar as Rawls's original position suggests that people are not morally responsible for many of their characteristics, including their willingness to work hard.

13. Edmund Burke, *Reflections on the Revolution in France* (Indianapolis: Hackett, 1987), 76.

14. Hayek, "The Origins and Effects of Our Morals," 318; Cass R. Sunstein, "Due Process Traditionalism," *Michigan Law Review* 106, no. 8 (2007): 1543–70. See also the discussion of the Condorcet jury theorem in Cass R. Sunstein, *Why Nudge? The Politics of Libertarian Paternalism* (New Haven, CT: Yale University Press, 2015).

15. To be sure, committed Burkeans, and some traditionalists, would have problems with that question. Pascal offered one response: "Those whom we call ancient were really new in all things, and properly constituted the infancy of mankind; and as we have joined to their knowledge the experience of the centuries which have followed them, it is in ourselves that we should find this antiquity that we revere in others." Blaise Pascal, "Preface to the Treatise on Vacuum," in *Thoughts, Letters, and Minor Works*, ed. Charles W. Eliot (New York: P. F. Collier, 1910), 449. Bentham similarly acknowledged that old people have more experience than young people, but insisted that "as between generation and generation, the reverse of this is true." Jeremy Bentham, *Handbook of Political Fallacies* (New York: Octagon Books, 1952), 44. In fact, he says, "The wisdom of the times called old" is "the wisdom of the cradle." Bentham deplored the "reigning prejudice in favor of the dead," and also the tendency to disparage the present generation, which has a greater stock of knowledge than "untaught, inexperienced generations."

NINE
"Who Will Stop Me?"

1. Ayn Rand, *The Fountainhead* (New York: New American Library, 1997).

2. Lisa Duggan, *Mean Girl: Ayn Rand and the Culture of Greed* (Oakland: University of California Press, 2019).

3. Ayn Rand, *Atlas Shrugged* (New York: New American Library, 1996).

4. "Paul Ryan and Ayn Rand," *New Republic*, December 28, 2010, https://newrepublic.com/article/80552/paul-ryan-and-ayn-rand.

5. See Jennifer Burns, *Goddess of the Market: Ayn Rand and the American Right* (Oxford: Oxford University Press, 2009).

6. Cass R. Sunstein, review of *Mean Girl: Ayn Rand and the Culture of Greed*, by Lisa Duggan, *New York Review of Books*, April 9, 2020, https://www.pressreader.com/usa/the-new-york-review-of-books/20200320/281573767763386.

7. "5 Things to Know about Frank O'Connor, Ayn Rand's Husband," *Atlas Society*, November 9, 2016, https://atlassociety.org/commentary/commentary-blog/6101-5-things-to-know-about-frank-o-connor-ayn-rand-s-husband.

8. Ayn Rand, "The Only Path to Tomorrow," Liberal Institute, http://www
.liberalinstitute.com/AynRand.html.
9. Sunstein, review of *Mean Girl.*
10. "Nathaniel Branden Dies at 84; Acolyte and Lover of Ayn Rand," *Los
Angeles Times*, December 9, 2014, https://www.latimes.com/local/obituaries
/la-me-nathaniel-branden-20141209-story.html.
11. Nathaniel Branden's *My Years with Ayn Rand* (San Francisco: Jossey-Bass,
1999) is a riveting account, lurid and full of insights. Excellent biographies,
offering far more detail than Duggan does, are Anne C. Heller, *Ayn Rand
and the World She Made* (New York: Anchor Books, 2009); and Burns,
Goddess of the Market.
12. Sunstein, review of *Mean Girl.*
13. Ibid.
14. Ibid.
15. Ibid.
16. Ibid.

TEN

History's Forks

1. The best treatment of this subject is Jon Elster, *Explaining Social Behavior*
(Cambridge: Cambridge University Press, 2015).
2. Jon Elster, *Logic and Society: Contradictions and Possible Worlds* (New York:
Wiley, 1978); David Lewis, *On the Plurality of Worlds* (Malden, MA:
Blackwell, 1986).
3. Richard J. Evans, *Altered Pasts: Counterfactuals in History* (Boston: Little,
Brown, 2014).
4. The classic text is H.L.A. Hart and Tony Honore, *Causation in the Law*
(Oxford: Clarendon, 1986).
5. Cass R. Sunstein, "What if Counterfactuals Never Existed?" *New Republic*,
September 20, 2014, https://newrepublic.com/article/119357/altered-pasts
-reviewed-cass-r-sunstein.
6. Ibid.
7. Philip E. Tetlock and Aaron Belkin, *Counterfactual Thought Experiments in
World Politics* (Princeton, NJ: Princeton University Press, 1996), 3.
8. Ibid., 17–32.
9. Robert Fogel, *Railroads and American Economic Growth* (Baltimore: Johns
Hopkins University Press, 1964).
10. See, for example, M. Hashem Pesaran and Ron P. Smith, "Counterfactual
Analysis in Macroeconometrics: An Empirical Investigation into the Effects
of Quantitative Easing," *Research in Economics* 70, no. 2 (2016): 262–80.
11. Sunstein, "What if Counterfactuals Never Existed?"

Acknowledgments

This short book is a product of many hands. I am grateful above all to my editor, Bill Frucht, for superb guidance at every stage. Sarah Chalfant, my agent, had faith in the project and the central thesis, even when I didn't. Conversations and collaborations with wonderful friends and coauthors were indispensable; special thanks to Elizabeth Emens, Dan Gilbert, Timur Kuran, Martha Nussbaum, Eric Posner, Robert Silvers, Richard Thaler, the late Edna Ullmann-Margalit, and Adrian Vermeule. Dinis Cheian provided superb research assistance.

A note about references: I have taken a minimalist approach here. For some quotations from books, I have referred to the books themselves, but not cluttered up the text with page references. Curious readers are invited to hunt. (It shouldn't be hard.)

I have drawn on previous publications here, though in all cases, there have been significant revisions. Special thanks to the

New York Review of Books for permissions to draw on materials originally published there for chapters 1, 5, 6, and 9: Cass R. Sunstein, "The Siren of Selfishness," *New York Review of Books*, April 9, 2020, https://www.nybooks.com/articles/2020/04/09 /ayn-rand-siren-selfishness/; Cass R. Sunstein, "It Can Happen Here," *New York Review of Books*, June 28, 2018, https://www .nybooks.com/articles/2018/06/28/hitlers-rise-it-can-happen -here/; Cass R. Sunstein, "The Refounding Father," *New York Review of Books*, June 5, 2014, https://www.nybooks.com/articles /2014/06/05/justice-stevens-refounding-father/; Cass R. Sunstein, "The Enlarged Republic—Then and Now," *New York Review of Books*, March 26, 2009, https://www.nybooks.com/articles /2009/03/26/the-enlarged-republicthen-and-now/. Thanks to the *University of Chicago Legal Forum* for permission to draw on materials originally published there for chapters 3 and 4: Cass R. Sunstein, "Lapidation and Apology," *University of Chicago Legal Forum* (forthcoming, 2020); Cass R. Sunstein, "#MeToo as a Revolutionary Cascade," *University of Chicago Legal Forum* (2019): 261. Thanks too to *American Affairs* for permission to draw on material originally published there for chapter 7: Cass R. Sunstein, "An Anatomy of Radicalism," *American Affairs* 2, no. 3 (Fall 2018): 64–77. I am grateful as well to the *Journal of Philosophy of History* for permission to draw on work originally published there for chapter 10: Cass R. Sunstein, "Historical Explanations Always Involve Counterfactual History," *Journal of the Philosophy of History* 10, no. 3 (2016): 433–40.

Warm thanks to Robin Charney for careful proofreading, to

Fred Kameny for preparing the index (and proofreading as well!), and to Joyce Ippolito for extraordinary work in bringing the book to completion. Special thanks too to Ron Giacoppo, Bianco Giacoppo, and my other friends at Club Car Cafe in West Concord, Massachusetts, where some of this book was written.

Index

Index

Index